THE
GLOSTERS
AN ILLUSTRATED HISTORY
OF A COUNTY REGIMENT

Men of D Company, 1st Battalion, having won the battalion cross-country championship in Dalhousie, India in 1908. Events such as these help foster the team spirit and comradeship which holds regiments together in battle.

THE
GLOSTERS
AN ILLUSTRATED HISTORY
OF A COUNTY REGIMENT

CHRISTOPHER NEWBOULD CBE
&
CHRISTINE BERESFORD BA MSocSc

First published in the United Kingdom in 1992 by
Alan Sutton Publishing Ltd · Phoenix Mill · Far Thrupp · Stroud ·
Gloucestershire

First published in the United States of America in 1993 by
Alan Sutton Publishing Inc. · Wolfeboro Falls · NH 03896–0484

British Library Cataloguing in Publication Data

Beresford, Christine
   Glosters: Illustrated History of a County
   Regiment
   I. Title   II. Newbould, Christopher
   355.3

ISBN 0-7509-0041-5

Typeset in Times 10/12.
Typesetting and origination by
Alan Sutton Publishing Limited.
Printed in Great Britain by
The Bath Press, Avon.

CONTENTS

ACKNOWLEDGEMENTS

We would like to acknowledge our debt to Major-General R.D. Grist OBE, Colonel The Gloucestershire Regiment, for his faith in this project which extended to unlimited access to the store-house of archival material housed in the Regimental Headquarters in Gloucester. We express our thanks to him and the trustees of The Gloucestershire Regiment collection for allowing us to reproduce the photographs in this book.

We are particularly grateful to the Regimental Secretary of the Glosters, Major Claud Rebbeck, whose comments and advice on the early drafts were invaluable. Any errors in this book are certainly not his. Brigadier Philip Heidenstam was another wise counsellor and his encouraging remarks on our early efforts were very important to us. Thanks are also due to the Honorary Archivist of The Gloucestershire Regiment, Lieutenant-Colonel Henry Radice, for his patience as we rummaged through his precious material and for his guidance on matters of detail.

We must also acknowledge our gratitude for the support of our respective spouses. Without their tolerant, good humoured acceptance of our prolonged preoccupation, to the exclusion of many of our domestic responsibilities, this book would not have been possible.

During the course of research for the text of the book we have drawn upon many sources, both published works and regimental archive material. They are listed in the bibliography which appears at the end of the book and source references are cited in the text for all quotations used.

Lastly, we pay tribute to all those past and present members of The Gloucestershire Regiment, both regular and territorial, and their relatives whose generous donation or loan of their photographic collections to the regiment created the foundations for the book.

The authors' royalties on this work are to be devoted to offset the running costs of the Regiments of Gloucestershire Museum, located at the Custom House in Gloucester Docks. In particular, we seek to provide for the conservation and care of the photographic material which was the source and inspiration for this book.

INTRODUCTION

The regiment known today as the Glosters was formed nearly 300 years ago. Their early exploits were recorded in narrative form and, on the rare occasions when they were illustrated, it was by water-colour or line engraving. Sometimes the more important battles were commemorated by grand oil paintings. In nearly every case, these early pictures allowed full rein to artistic interpretation. Soldiers fought in bright clean uniforms and faced the enemy with heroic, determined expressions on their faces. Mud and gore were invariably absent.

Sometimes senior officers, who in reality were nowhere near the fighting, were portrayed in glorious motion at the head of their troops in contact with the enemy. Indeed, it is said that some of the characters appearing in Benjamin West's famous painting of the death of Wolfe at Quebec in 1759 paid the artist so that they might be included in the scene.

Elsewhere, while some participants were talented artists, they were usually too preoccupied with their duties to record the action at the time. One is thus dependent upon their memories and sketches drawn before or after the great events.[1]

The invention of the camera in the middle of the nineteenth century changed all that. For the first time, it was possible to capture images of people as they really were, rather than as a romantic illustrator thought they should be. The growing demands of newspapers and other illustrated publications led to an insatiable demand for photographs. Queen Victoria's army was perpetually involved in military adventures of one sort or another and public interest in their deeds was endless. To begin with, the line engravings produced by graphic illustrators had the monopoly. It was not long, however, before photographic enthusiasts realized that life at the front offered fertile ground for the new medium. Most of the earlier pictures were simple portraits. The long exposure times needed precluded the more mobile action shots that would become commonplace in the twentieth century. Fortunately, the subjects did not mind; soldiers have never been reluctant to have their pictures taken. Their simple pleasure in posing for photographs links the generations over the years.

This book is devoted to the photographs preserved in the archives of The Gloucestershire Regiment and spans the century from the Crimean War in 1854 to the campaign fought in Korea between 1950 and 1951. Most of the photographs are from albums which were maintained by the various battalions of the regiment; others originate from personal collections. Initially, the pictures are few, reflecting

Proud Gilbert Harding in his new uniform, aged 16. It is August 1914 and he has just enlisted in the 6th Glosters by lying about his age. Soon he will be in France with the British Expeditionary Force. Before reaching his 19th birthday, he will be one of the 8,100 Glosters who gave their lives during the First World War. He was killed in action with the 12th Glosters (Bristol's Own) at Vimy Ridge in April 1917.

the specialist nature of the art. As technology made the camera more accessible, portable and easier to operate, so interest in photography blossomed. By the 1930s the Brownie box camera was available and soldiers could take their own pictures, both for their own scrapbooks and for their families. There are several poignant examples in these pages. By the time of the Second World War there were specialist photo-journalists and public relations teams who were able to capture every facet of military life on film. Some of the work of those who followed the Glosters into action is recorded in this book.

Our selections from this rich source of material are organized into themes which illustrate various aspects of soldiering in the Glosters over a hundred years. At home and abroad, at work or play, in peace and war – small fragments of the rich tapestry of regimental life which, for those who have experienced it, is like none other. It would be fitting if, in 2050, there were another volume to take the story into the twenty-first century. If so, the book could have a different title, for in 1994, after 300 years of loyal service to Crown and Country, the Glosters are due to amalgamate with the Duke of Edinburgh's Royal Regiment to form a new Royal Gloucestershire, Berkshire and Wiltshire Regiment. For those who know and love the Glosters, this is a great sadness but it is not the first time their name has changed. Raised as Gibson's Regiment of Foot in 1694, they have known many titles over the centuries. Nevertheless, their spirit has endured and is typified by the words spoken by one Colonel of the Regiment on a parade when he was irritated by the strange titles other regiments used:

Neither King's nor Queen's nor Royal Marines!
But 28th, Old Bragg's;
Brass before and Brass behind
– Ne'er feared a foe of any kind!
Shoulder Arms!

The cross country, obstacle and relay teams of E Company, 2nd Battalion, in Malta in 1913.
Some eighteen months later, these fit and well-trained men were under fire in the trenches in France.

Chapter 1
THE REGIMENT BEFORE THE CAMERA: 1694–1850

The soldier is a peculiar being that can alone be brought to the highest efficiency by inducing him to believe that he belongs to a regiment that is infinitely superior to the others around him.

Field Marshal Viscount Wolseley
The Soldiers Pocket Book (1869)

The loneliest place on earth for the foot soldier is the battlefield. It was ever thus. Cavalry, artillery and others have always been able to draw comfort from their horses, tanks or guns to sustain them when they are afraid. In more modern times, RAF jet pilots who fought against Iraq in the Gulf War of 1991, when asked how they felt when pressing home their attacks against strong enemy missile defences, said that they were too busy flying their aeroplanes to think about it. Certainly, unless they are prepared to eject, it is difficult for pilots to run away.

This is not to denigrate the skill and determination needed by members of other arms in battle, but the situation of the infantryman is singularly different. Alone among the fighting services, the infantryman can always find a reason to convince himself that his individual actions will not influence the outcome of a battle. Lying in a shallow trench or shell scrape, out of sight of his comrades, it would be easy for him to keep his head down, avoid risk and hide until things died down. That he rarely does so, at least in the case of the British Army, is a tribute to the strength of his loyalty to his comrades, men whom he knows and trusts. He knows that if he is to survive the dangers and horrors of war, he needs the support of his friends – just as they need his. This small group loyalty is strengthened by the pride of the well disciplined soldier who, more than anything else, fears the loss of 'his reputation as a man amongst men'[1] if he were to fail his friends in their hour of need. It has always been the well founded belief of the British Army that such loyalties are easier to develop if all the members of a unit come from the same part of the country. Thus small groups or sections of men are formed into platoons and companies to make up a battalion of a regiment. For the long service, regular, volunteer soldier the regiment becomes his family. So it is with the Glosters. Every member of the regiment knows, with a certainty that defies contradiction, that they are superior to any other, an élite and exclusive club, the membership of which must be earned.

5

The regiment is a close-knit network of friends and comrades who draw comfort from each other's presence and the example of their forebears over the years. Their traditions are enshrined in their cap badge and the honours and reputation earned in battle by those who went before them. They engender a pride which the regiment will defend fiercely against all comers in battle, on the playing field or anywhere else.

Every regiment develops its own unique style or character. The Glosters' roots are deep in the soil of towns and villages in the Cotswolds, the Forest of Dean and the Severn Vale. Many of them were, and are still, men from the old port of Bristol, with a smattering of Welsh and Irish to leaven the bread. It is a corner of England renowned for men of character, ready to answer the call to serve in their local regiment. Sturdy, independent individuals with a soft gentle tongue who are slow to anger but fight like the devil when roused. Their dogged determination and ability to endure privation and hardship have been tested many times over the years.

The Glosters were raised in Portsmouth in March 1694 to fight against the French. They took their name from the man who raised and first commanded them, Colonel John Gibson. Every man was a volunteer. They joined for different reasons; some for the bounty paid to recruits, others to escape the law or unexpected family responsibilities. Some were undoubtedly attracted by the uniform and tales of adventure in foreign parts. For many it was probably the prospect of a square meal and warm clothing; times were hard in England in those days. Beginning in the eighteenth century, the Industrial Revolution created an

Former members of The Gloucestershire Regiment gather at the Regimental Depot, Horfield Barracks, Bristol, for Old Soldiers' Day, 1932.

Some idea of the economic conditions prevailing before the Second World War is given in these pictures of new recruits during their training at the regimental depot, in 1931. The top photograph was taken on the day of enlistment; the second after eight weeks' training. By the end of their training, they had gained an average of a stone in weight and expanded their chest measurements by two inches.

urban working class. Poor working conditions in the new factories combined with agricultural recession to create unemployment and starvation which produced many recruits for the new regiment. Recruiting often improved during the hard winter months when Jack Frost was said to be the best recruiting sergeant the Army had.

At first, the Colonel clothed and paid for his men out of a grant from the Government, frequently managing to make a profit. Further money could be made from the sale of the regiment and, over the years, as colonels changed, so did the regiment's name. Thus Gibson's became De Lalo's, then Mordaunt's and subsequently Bragg's. Whatever their name they fought, usually against the French, wherever duty called. In 1742 they were given the title '28th Foot' to indicate their seniority amongst other infantry regiments.

THE COLOURS

The pride and soul of a regiment lies in its Colours; two flags made of silk, of which one symbolizes the Union, and is known as the King's or Queen's Colour. The other is the Regimental Colour, made of the same shade as that

In the early years of the regiment the colonel paid for his soldiers' clothes out of a government grant. Men of the 28th at the Woolwich Tattoo of 1930 are wearing examples of the red coats which were worn in the first half of the eighteenth century.

worn on the cuffs and facings of the soldiers' uniforms. Initially painted, but later intricately embroidered, the Colours came to bear the names of the battles in which the regiment had distinguished itself. In early times the Colours acted as a rallying point in battle. For as long as they were visible they marked the location of the Colonel and signified that the regiment was an effective fighting force.

Later in the eighteenth century, as a response to the continuing threat from France, the army expanded and other regiments were formed – including the 61st Foot. In 1782, for recruiting purposes, the 28th and the 61st became respectively the North and South Gloucestershire Regiments. Among other places they saw service in Canada, where the 28th were amongst the first troops to scale the Heights of Abraham under General Wolfe at Quebec in 1759. They also saw action in North America against the rebel colonists, where they were undefeated, and subsequently in the West Indies, when France joined the war.

THE WAR AGAINST NAPOLEONIC FRANCE

Both regiments distinguished themselves during the Napoleonic wars. The most significant moment in the history of the 28th Regiment took place in Egypt which Napoleon had invaded in 1798, posing a threat to the British position in India. Britain could not permit this and the French army were first isolated by Nelson's naval victory at the Battle of the Nile. A British army, which included the 28th, was

A moth eaten rag on a worm eaten pole,
It does not look likely to stir a man's soul
'Tis the deeds that were done 'neath the moth eaten rag
When the pole was a staff, and the rag was a flag.

Part of the Regimental Colour of the 61st Foot, later 2nd Battalion, The Gloucestershire Regiment. It bears the sphinx awarded as a battle honour for their part in the Egyptian Campaign of 1801 against the French. This Colour was carried by the regiment between 1816 and 1828. To this day, the Colours are treasured items which are always treated with respect and veneration. When on parade, soldiers salute and members of the public are expected to stand as the Colours pass by.

then sent to evict the invaders and landed near Alexandria in March 1801. The crucial moment in the campaign came a few days later on 21 March. In a dawn attack, the French nearly succeeded in overcoming the British force when they broke through their lines and attacked from front and rear simultaneously at a key point held by the 28th.

The regiment stood and fought, back to back, in a ferocious battle which lasted for some hours. The French suffered heavy casualties, failed to overcome the 28th and finally withdrew leaving the British victors in the field and masters of Egypt. It was the first real success by the British Army in the war. As a result of their part in the battle, the 28th earned the right to wear their badge on the back of their caps as well as at the front – the only regiment in the British Army

A Victorian view of the sphinx, symbol of the fierce struggle by the 28th at the battle of Alexandria in 1801, where they earned the right to wear a badge on the back of their head-dress as well as the front. This photograph was taken by a member of the 28th based at Alexandria in 1895. The sphinx looks very different today.

to be permitted to do so. This was the origin of the famous back badge worn by the Glosters today.

Between 1809 and 1814 both the 28th and the 61st helped to drive the French armies from Spain, in a series of hard-fought actions under the command of the Duke of Wellington. Michael Barthorp in his *Armies of Britain* describes the achievement thus:

> Ultimately the system and the tactics, the victories, sieges, advances and retreats depended above all on the quality of the regiments of the Line, in their battered shakos, faded red jackets and ragged trousers, weighed down by knapsack, pouch and musket; marching, fighting and enduring across blazing sierras, snow covered mountains and in flea-ridden villages. The years of campaigning welded together a collection of regiments into a powerful and cohesive force, with a spirited, aggressive and self-confident character of its own.
>
> An arduous open-air life and shared dangers narrowed the divisions between the ranks; on the one hand the officers, sons of the gentry and professional classes, boys just out of school, ageing captains too poor to buy their pro-motion, offspring of rich tradesmen, quarrelsome squireens . . . ; on the other the rank and file, ploughboys, jailbirds, riotous Irish, well set-up militiamen, out of work weavers, pale-faced youths from the new slums, most of them illiterate but a surprising number with some education, and almost all with a bottomless capacity for drink; between the two, the real professionals, the sergeants, hard tough and experienced, guiding the young officers and ever watchful of the men.[2]

The campaign medal on the left is for Military General Service. It was issued to reward Wellington's troops for their victories during the Napoleonic War. It bears the clasp for the Egyptian campaign of 1801, others were issued for different battles. The medal was not created until 1847 because, it is said, the Duke of Wellington objected to soldiers being issued with medals. By then, Queen Victoria was on the throne, but there were few survivors alive to receive it. The Sultan's Gold Medal on the right was issued to officers only.

Barthorp points out that what cemented officers and men together was regimental pride, 'a determination to uphold the honour of what for many of them was the only home they knew'. As an example of this extraordinary pride which sustained men throughout the campaign, he tells the story of Sergeant Ball of the 28th. Together with a fatigue party of two men, Sergeant Ball happened to arrive at a British camp to hear that an assault was being planned upon San Sebastian. He promptly decided to take part since, as he said in a letter afterwards, 'there was hardly an action in the Peninsula in which the 28th had not had a share'.[3] This small incident typifies the regimental spirit of The Gloucestershire Regiment and the pride that all ranks take in maintaining their reputation.

By the time Napoleon abdicated in April 1814, both regiments had gained fifteen battle honours to be emblazoned on their Colours.[4] However, peace did not last long. Napoleon escaped from Elba and was confronted by Wellington at Waterloo in June 1815. The day before, at Quatre Bras, the 28th had helped to halt Napoleon's advance guard. At the main battle it formed the centre of the British line and afterwards was the only English regiment to be singled out for mention in Wellington's famous Waterloo despatch. In the two days, Quatre Bras and Waterloo, the 28th lost 250 officers and soldiers in killed and wounded, two-fifths of its total strength. It was a high price to pay for the years of peace which were to follow. Those who survived the battle were permitted to count two years' service towards pension.

At the end of the Napoleonic War, the 28th and the 61st had reached a peak of military efficiency. Hardened by years of campaigning they had an enviable record which laid the foundations for the years of service which were to follow. However, the British have always been an unmilitary nation and with the threat of invasion removed, interest in the army lapsed. As the seventeenth-century poet Francis Quarles remarked:

> Our God and soldiers we alike adore
> Ev'n at the brink of danger; not before:
> After deliverance, both alike requited,
> Our God's forgotten, and our soldiers slighted.

For the next forty years the army entered a period of stagnation and neglect which continued until the outbreak of the Crimean War in 1854.

Chapter 2

THE SOLDIER AND THE TOOLS OF HIS TRADE

I have never been able to join in the popular cry about the recklessness, sensuality and helplessness of the soldiers. On the contrary I should say that I have never seen so teachable and helpful a class as the Army generally. Give them opportunity promptly and securely to send money home and they will use it. Give them schools and lectures and they will come to use them. Give them books and games and amusements and they will leave off drinking. Give them suffering and they will bear it. Give them work and they will do it.

Florence Nightingale, in a letter to her sister (March 1856)[1]

The camera first came into its own in mid-Victorian times. By then, the Industrial Revolution and the great period of Victorian invention and enterprise were well under way. However, the recruit who joined the 28th or the 61st in the 1850s would have found it little changed since the end of the Napoleonic War in 1815. The pay was the same, around a shilling a day, but the average soldier was lucky if he saw much of it. By the time deductions had been made for food and the upkeep of kit, he was lucky if he had a few pence left over. More often than not he was in debt.

UNIFORMS

The soldier's uniform included a thick scarlet jacket made of serge, from factories such as those in the valleys around Stroud. In winter he wore blue woollen trousers replaced by white linen in summer. A bell-topped shako of felt was more decorative than useful. His wardrobe was completed by pipe-clayed leather equipment including a knapsack in which to keep his few belongings and a blanket. In 1843, left and right ankle boots were issued for the first time. Before that, soldiers were required to change their boots from one foot to another each day to even out the wear!

Barracks were plain, poorly ventilated and cramped. There was no central heating or privacy in this 1913 barrack room of the 61st in Tientsin, China, home for twenty or thirty men. In the narrow confines of this picture two soldiers lived when off duty. To encourage tidiness and to ensure that their equipment was serviceable, soldiers were required to lay out their kit

for inspection at regular intervals. When not in use, all their belongings would be stowed away in the foot lockers in the foreground. A small bird cage and a few personal photographs add a touch of domesticity.

The bell tent was standard accommodation for the army in the field for well over 100 years. Men slept on bare boards, with two blankets each and their feet pointing towards the tent pole. The stacked tea mugs show that this tent held ten men. The label on the pole lists the roll of the occupants, in this case men of the 4th Battalion, camping in Cirencester Park sometime between 1881 and 1890. Their communal water bucket is on the right.

BARRACKS

The soldier lived in a plain, poorly ventilated and cramped barrack room with twenty or thirty other men, women and children.[2] Hygiene and sanitary facilities were appalling. The first bath in an English barracks was not built until 1855. The diet was monotonous: two meals a day – usually consisting of boiled beef, vegetables and bread. The food was cooked by the soldiers themselves, who took turns to prepare meals for the men in their barrack room. The working day began with Reveille sounded on the bugles that regulated the regiment's life. From Reveille until lights out, bugles would sound in barracks at regular intervals. They summoned men to fall in, report for fatigues or meals, collect the mail, parade for guard and many other routine duties. Each bugle call was known to the men by words put to the tune, some of which were unprintable.

BOREDOM

There were no recreational or sporting facilities, and in the evenings time lay heavy on their hands. Education for soldiers was regarded as highly dangerous, bringing with it the risk of subversive propaganda spreading dissent in the ranks.[3] Boredom was the real enemy, and it is not surprising that many turned to drink. Gin was cheap and plentiful; beer was usually too expensive.

DISCIPLINE

Discipline was strict although flogging was reserved for more serious crimes. Fortunately the average soldier was of hardy stock; he had to be to survive. Even so, disease claimed more victims than enemy action, particularly overseas where cholera, dysentery and yellow fever took their toll.

CONDITIONS OF SERVICE

The 28th had also served in India but in 1854 they joined the Allied British and French force which set sail for the Crimea to thwart Russian designs on Turkey. The regiment performed creditably at Sebastopol, Alma and Inkerman but the campaign revealed weaknesses in an army that had seen no major war for forty years. Administrative inefficiency was rife and many of the hardships suffered by the soldiers could have been avoided. The scandalous arrangements for casualties, publicized by Florence Nightingale and W.H. Russell of *The Times* provoked a public outcry. Slowly conditions of service improved.

WEAPONS

In the 1850s the muzzle-loading Lee Enfield rifle replaced the Brown Bess musket which had been in use for over a hundred years. The introduction of an accurate weapon with a range of several hundred yards was an important change. It meant an end to the old practice of densely packed troops standing in line or forming squares, whilst firing disciplined volleys to repel enemy attacks. When success in battle depended upon volley firing, the soldier rarely had to think for himself. Indeed, he was positively discouraged from doing so and his 100-man company would be drilled until each man reacted automatically, as if part of a well-oiled machine. He marched, halted and fired his musket on command. If he was pointed to the front, he was sure to hit something. The arrival of the rifle made it possible for soldiers to engage distant targets instead of waiting until they could see the whites of the enemy's eyes.

Of course, the widespread introduction of the rifle also meant that the soldier himself was liable to be shot at from a distance. As the nineteenth century wore on, so the accuracy of all weapons improved and the devastating effect of enemy rifle fire during the Boer War in South Africa in 1899 demonstrated the necessity for soldiers to operate in more dispersed formations. In turn, this made it more difficult for them to be controlled centrally by word of mouth. Self discipline became more important, and soldiers were encouraged to think and act independently in a way which would have amazed many Napoleonic veterans.

ARMY REFORM

Whereas in 1801 the soldier was encouraged with rum and loot or coerced by the lash, from 1881 onwards a minor revolution took place. Discipline was still strict

A re-enactment of eighteenth-century military punishments for the 1926 Woolwich Military Tattoo. Flogging was not finally abolished until 1881 after much controversial public debate.

but the carrot became more important than the stick. Corporal punishment was abolished and minor infringements were dealt with by confinement to barracks or forfeiture of pay, a practice which continues to this day. It was found that more than 60 per cent of soldiers were illiterate, and a fledgling army education service was formed. The system of officers purchasing their commissions was abolished and the quality of professional leadership improved. Training gave more emphasis to individual skills, including shooting and skirmishing.

Barracks were improved, and recreation and dining rooms were built. By 1900, soldiers enjoyed three meals a day, prepared by regimental cooks. Even plumbing was installed. There was more than a hint of reform in the air! Dry canteens were introduced where soldiers could buy tea or coffee as an alternative to the spirits available in the 'wet' canteen. Even so, life in barracks would remain a spartan existence for many years. One soldier who joined the 28th in 1919 reports:

I joined the 28th in Maidstone. We were in civilian billets and I, with five others, were unlucky in our place, as the landladies were paid sixpence per day for each soldier and were required to provide only a room in which to sleep and morning washing facilities and, my word, our landlady kept to her contract – we slept on

the floor, with no light (we bought candles), and the washing facilities were a bucket of water in the yard.

Later we moved to Catterick, in the hutted camp. Here we slept on bed boards raised six inches off the floor by trestles and had a paliasse filled with straw,[4] which we changed once a month.[5]

During the late nineteenth century, uniforms gradually became more comfortable and practical. The red jackets which, with their white cross belts, made such prominent aiming marks in battle disappeared for all except ceremonial use. The 61st in India in 1857 had been one of the first regiments to dye their tropical uniforms a light brown colour known by the native word for dust – khaki. For infantry regiments who spent so much of their time on the march, the appearance of better quality boots – not to mention socks – was another welcome improvement.

1881 was a milestone for the 28th and the 61st Foot in other ways. In that year, they were combined to form the 1st and 2nd Battalions of The Gloucestershire Regiment.[6] The design of the back badge was changed from the regimental number to a sphinx on a pedestal inscribed 'Egypt', within a laurel wreath. This badge is worn to this day.

In 1931, the 28th played a prominent part in the Royal Tournament at Olympia. Here a scene from the Crimean War of 1854 is re-enacted. These tight-fitting Victorian coatees and cumbersome caps were not practical fighting garments. They were uncomfortable to fight in and gave little protection from the elements or the enemy. Although designs would soon improve, it would be some time before the scarlet jacket disappeared from the military scene.

THE AMALGAMATION OF THE 28TH AND 61ST

After the Second World War it was decided to reduce the size of infantry regiments from two battalions to one. In 1948, in Jamaica, the two regular battalions of the regiment were amalgamated and became the 1st Battalion, The Gloucestershire Regiment (28th/61st).

NEW EQUIPMENT

In the 1860s and '70s the breech-loading rifle replaced the muzzle loader and it was no longer necessary for men to pour powder and ball into the barrel and drive them home with a ramrod. By the early 1900s smokeless powder and metal cartridges were in service, together with a bolt-action rifle which enabled the well-trained rifleman to produce a rapid rate of fire of fifteen rounds a minute. By 1914, at the beginning of the First World War, the marksmanship of the army had improved so much that the Germans thought they were being engaged by machine-guns, whereas in fact these were few and far between.

The use of the machine-gun, known as 'concentrated essence of infantry', soon became widespread in the First World War. It combined with the devastating effects of modern artillery to produce a stalemate and the trench warfare which led to further developments in equipment and weaponry. The steel helmet and the grenade, which had been a feature of war as far back as medieval times, were rediscovered. In the final year of the war, men of the Glosters in common with the rest of the army learned to fight in close knit teams with supporting fire from tanks and artillery.

Between the two World Wars advancing technology had more dramatic effects upon the tools of the Glosters' trade. By 1937, both battalions were equipped with machine-guns and rudimentary anti-tank weapons. As the Second World War continued, so the proportion of automatic weapons to rifles increased. Small, portable anti-tank weapons arrived, such as the PIAT – or Projector Infantry Anti-Tank. Assisted by their wheeled anti-tank guns, infantry battalions could now produce some sort of defence against enemy armour. Each battalion was issued with 3-inch mortars, their near-vertical trajectories enabling attacks to be made upon enemy troops and soft-skinned vehicles hiding behind cover.

By now, wireless communication between companies was slowly replacing field telephones and the archaic semaphore flags and mirrors of the previous century. At the outbreak of the Second World War, both battalions had some men mechanized in tracked, armoured carriers. However, the carriers were few and their cross-country performance was limited. Even as late as 1950 when the Glosters went to Korea with the United Nations Forces, the average infantryman was still dependent upon his ability to march and carry his pack and his personal weapon just as he had done on the road to Waterloo in 1815.

Annual camp is an important milestone in the training year for part-time soldiers of the Territorial Army. Here men of the 5th Glosters prepare to move off to the rifle range somewhere on Salisbury Plain in 1910.

Major Benson of the 28th wearing high spurred boots polished to a glassy sheen, blue breeches with a red stripe and a scarlet jacket, photographed in 1897. The more comfortable side hat suggests that he may have just come off parade and removed his formal headgear. Although all officers were expected to be able to ride, only the commanding officer, second-in-command, adjutant and signal officer were normally mounted on parade. Other officers rode when their duties required it.

Major Archdale, Adjutant of the regimental depot at Horfield Barracks in Bristol in 1890, receives a haircut from the regimental barber. The tents would have been used for training by recruits and the local Volunteers.

From 1881 until the early 1900s, the badge worn on caps of the Glosters included the arms of the City of Gloucester in red enamel beneath a gilt sphinx. Above left, Major M.E. Archdale of the 61st is shown, c. 1893.

Lieutenant A.C. Lovett (above right) was a distinguished water-colour artist who specialized in painting the uniforms of the Indian Army. He is dressed in the full ceremonial scarlet tunic, which was worn until the Second World War. He was promoted to Lieutenant Colonel in 1911, took the 28th to France in 1914 and subsequently retired as a Brigadier General. His son, Nigel, followed him into the regiment and was also an accomplished artist. The photograph dates from 1883.

Private P.E. Pugh poses for a family snap in his barrack room before the First World War. He is wearing his uniform shirt; pyjamas were rarely worn and were certainly not issued in those days. His shaving gear and eating irons are secured to the lid of his foot locker. His leather ammunition pouches, bayonet and water bottle hang neatly behind him. Private Pugh ran away from home in Bristol to join the 2nd Battalion as a drummer in 1907 and served for nearly twelve years.

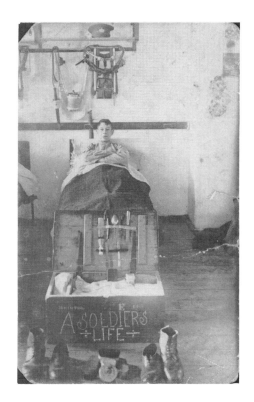

The Sergeants' Mess of the 1st Battalion, Mustapha Pasha Barracks, Alexandria, in 1896. Lofty barrack blocks with cool verandahs became a feature of Victorian military architecture abroad.

The Officers' Mess, 1st Battalion, Mustapha Pasha Barracks. The Officers' Mess was usually built in a secluded spot away from the men's accommodation, a convenient arrangement for both parties.

Until after the Second World War, many soldiers slept on straw-filled paliasses. Here men of the 3rd Battalion collect their straw at the start of annual camp, 1907.

The Cyclist Corps: Bristol Volunteers in 1901. The arrival of a reliable, mass-produced bicycle in the early twentieth century was seen by some as a major military advance with its potential for fast, silent movement. Lack of roads and the arrival of the machine-gun limited its use to administrative duties behind the front line. The pattern of side hat worn by the men is still in use today.

The 61st was among the first battalions to wear Khaki uniforms in India in 1857. Khaki blended with sandy landscapes and was less obvious than scarlet. However, looser fitting, more comfortable and practical uniforms did not become commonplace until the late nineteenth century. Here three Volunteer officers attached to the 61st are dressed for campaign service in South Africa during the Boer War of 1899–1901. During the war the back badge was represented by a piece of red cloth embroidered with 'GLOSTER'.

The development of an efficient automatic machine-gun by the American inventor Hiram Maxim in the late nineteenth century transformed modern warfare. Sadly its potential was better exploited by other countries at Britain's expense during the First World War. Only two guns per battalion were issued to British Infantry, shown here with the 61st in Malta in 1913.

Not until the army was mechanized in the 1930s was motor transport widely available. Until then, horse- and mule-drawn wagons were used for all purposes. Shown here are those of the 3rd Battalion at camp in 1916.

The photograph shows regimental depot officers at Horfield Barracks, Bristol, in 1927. Maj. A.C. Vicary DSO, MC (Depot Commander) is in the centre. Left to right: Capt. W.H. Hynes (Adjutant), Capt. R.B. James, Capt. R. Power OBE, Lt. G.W.V. Ladds, Lt. J.W.C. Kirkland. From 1902 until 1940, the British Army officers' uniform for most purposes except ceremonial was known as service dress. The depot commander and adjutant were mounted, hence their breeches. Most of the officers wear medal ribbons from the First World War.

A territorial battalion of the regiment at Annual Camp, Portsmouth, 1920. After the First World War the reserve units of the regiment were reduced to three territorial battalions. The 3rd Battalion was disbanded in 1922, leaving the 4th, 5th and 6th Glosters. Here territorials of the Glosters parade with their band and drums during their annual training period. Their tents have clearly seen better days, but between the wars there was little money to spare for re-equipping the army.

A Crimean War veteran chats to a
territorial band boy (4ft 7in tall) and
a Regular Gloster (6ft 6in) at a 1931
Old Soldiers' Day in Horfield
Barracks.

The Lewis light machine-gun with its distinctive drum magazine was the first issued to the
British Army and is shown here in Egypt, in 1936. The mainstay of battalion defences in the
trenches between 1914 and 1918, its complex mechanism made it liable to regular misfire.
When it did so, the training manual listed eighteen possible causes. The Lewis gun remained
in service until the outbreak of the Second World War, when it was replaced by the Bren
gun. Soldiers from the 2nd Battalion are shown photographed wearing the back badge on
their steel helmets.

The introduction of the Bren light machine-gun in the early years of the Second World War was a major advance. It allowed soldiers to manoeuvre and attack rapidly with their own covering fire. It proved to be a most reliable, accurate and efficient gun which could, if necessary, be fired on the move. Those who used it had great confidence in its capabilities. In the foreground is the tripod which provided a stable platform for the Bren in defensive positions or for use against aircraft. The photograph was taken in Burma, in June 1941.

Early Signallers in South Africa, 1900. For most of the Victorian era, military messages were sent over long distances in morse code by reflected sunlight in the mirrors of the heliograph. The system was less effective under cloudy European skies.

The signallers of the 28th with their heliographs, lamps, telescopes and signalling flags in the days before the advent of the wireless, photographed in Ceylon, *c.* 1902.

The 2nd Battalion became a mechanized machine-gun battalion in 1937. Three of the four rifle companies were mounted in Bren gun carriers (shown on the right). The fourth company was equipped with anti-tank guns (centre) and rode in half-ton trucks (left). For a battalion accustomed to marching nearly everywhere, the scale of the change-over was dramatic, as they learned to cope with the unfamiliar daily maintenance of these vehicles. In the foreground are the Boyes anti-tank rifle, a Vickers machine-gun and the Bren gun. In June 1939, the War Office had second thoughts and the battalion reverted to dismounted infantry.

The introduction of battledress in 1940 was greeted with mixed feelings by old soldiers. Designed to be a practical, loose-fitting dress for both barracks and active service, it was based upon ski-suits of the time. Although there were no buttons to be polished, the heavy serge cloth required much time on the ironing board to keep it smart. Here, young soldiers of the Glosters under training at the Wessex Infantry Training centre, are putting on a display at the Bath & West Show in Cheltenham, in May 1947. Battledress was worn throughout the Second World War and in Korea, finally disappearing in the mid-1960s.

Scenes such as these at the 6th Battalion's camp around 1911 were a familiar feature of training before and after the First World War. Most moves were on foot, and training was based upon the ability to march long distances while remaining fit to fight at the end of the day.

Chapter 3

CEREMONIAL, TRADITION AND LOYALTY

No one who has participated in it or seen it well done should doubt the inspiration of ceremonial drill.

Field Marshal Earl Wavell
The Good Soldier (1948)

Every trifle, every tag or ribbon that tradition may have associated with the former glories of a regiment should be retained, so long as its retention does not interfere with efficiency.

Colonel Clifford Walton
History of the British Standing Army, 1660–1700 (1894)

DRILL

Drill on the barrack square has long been an important feature of regimental life in the British Army, although its purpose is often misunderstood. Even though drill is no longer the dominant feature of a soldier's day, there are many special regimental occasions, such as the anniversaries of important battles, which are commemorated by parades. In the case of the Glosters, the battles of Alexandria (21 March) Salamanca (22 July) or Imjin (25 April) are often marked by the officers and men of the 1st Battalion who parade with their Colours, the regimental band and the Corps of Drums. To any who have served, and many of their families too, it is always a stirring sight to see the ranks of soldiers, the sunlight glistening on their bayonets and the silk of the Colours fluttering in the breeze whilst the battalion march on parade, as they always do, to the tune of 'Army of the Nile'.

The modern onlooker, unversed in military matters, might think that such displays were mere theatricals, with no practical purpose. Few soldiers would agree for, to them, a parade is the outward and visible display of their regimental pride in themselves and the achievements of their predecessors over the centuries – guaranteed to uplift the spirit and impress the ladies!

In earlier times the intricate manoeuvres seen on the parade ground fulfilled a more serious purpose on the battlefield. Above all, the constant repetition of the

The 1st Battalion on parade in Wellington, India in 1937 to celebrate the King's birthday. Wherever the army serves, the sovereign's birthday is usually celebrated with a full

ceremonial parade. Many hours are spent preparing and rehearsing.

drill movements meant that men could carry them out instinctively – especially when they were frightened and wished to be somewhere else. Drilling together forced new recruits to think and act as one body rather than as undisciplined individuals. In learning this, they began to understand the importance of teamwork. So the bonds of comradeship and discipline developed which enabled the 28th to withstand the charges of Napoleon's cavalry and infantry at Alexandria in 1801. Teamwork is so important to effective soldiering that drill is still part of a modern recruit's training.

The value of well-rehearsed drills is not confined to the barrack square and is equally applicable to the handling of modern weapons and equipment. The difficulty is to inculcate sensible discipline, without destroying individual initiative. Fortunately the sturdy, independent spirit of the British soldier is his best safeguard against the cult of mindless obedience which has sometimes afflicted other armies.

THE COLOURS ON PARADE

The best-known parade ground ceremony is that of Trooping the Colour. Held annually on Horse Guards Parade in honour of the Queen's birthday, its origins lie

Dressed in full ceremonial scarlet, B Company, 1st Battalion march past the inspecting officer with bayonets fixed and eyes right at the King's Birthday Parade in Bordon, June 1914.

on the battlefields of yesteryear. It was then the custom, before an action, to parade the Colours, or 'troop' them, before the soldiers so that all would recognize them, not only as a symbol of the honour of the regiment, but as a practical marker of the headquarters' location in the heat of battle. The Colours were at the heart of the 28th Foot at Waterloo, where the silk was tattered and torn by enemy musket balls and the pikes shattered.

Traditionally, the Colours are always carried by two junior officers with an escort of Colour Sergeants. The widespread use of rifles after the Napoleonic War made Colour parties an easy target, and the last time the Colours were carried in action by the regiment was in 1854 at the battle of the Alma during the Crimean War. Today, the Queen's Colour is only carried in the presence of a member or representative of the Royal family, or a foreign head of state. When not on parade, the Colours are housed in the Officers' Mess.

The Colours themselves are works of art, once probably hand stitched by nimble seamstresses and repaired by regimental wives. More recently they were embroidered by professionals such as those of the Royal School of Needlework. The Regimental Colour in particular is a source of great pride since it bears the unique distinctions of The Gloucestershire Regiment. Originally both the 28th and the 61st

Back Badge Day, 1932. The Regimental Colour of the 61st and its Escort march past the Colonel of the regiment, Brigadier-General A.W. Pagan, DSO. The only occasion when the Colour is allowed to fly freely is when saluting the inspecting officer. At other times, to protect it from damage, the young officer, or Ensign, holds the silk of the Colour securely in his hand.

In the early years of the century, soldiers of the 61st practise their bayonet drill under the eagle eye of their sergeant.

had separate colours, each matching the regimental facings worn on their tunics –
yellow for the 28th and buff for the 61st.

BATTLE HONOURS

The practice of bearing battle honours on the Colours dates from 1768. Governed
by strict rules laid down by the War Office (now the Ministry of Defence),
permission to bear an honour is reserved for those regiments who distinguished
themselves in the battle concerned. Before the spate of amalgamations after the
Second World War, the Glosters could state with pride that their Regimental
Colour bore more battle honours than that of any other regiment.

The first honour to be carried was the word 'Egypt' under a sphinx within a laurel
wreath in commemoration of the 1801 campaign. Subsequently the regiment was

The amalgamation of the 28th and 61st, Kingston, Jamaica, 21 September 1948. The climax
of the amalgamation parade was the trooping of the 28th Colours around the amalgamated
battalion. The King's Colour is carried by Captain T.A.K. Dillon and the Regimental
Colour by Captain W.A. Wood. The Colours seen here were presented to the 28th or North
Gloucestershire Regiment in 1868. They headed the 1st Battalion into Germany at the end
of the Great War in 1918. In 1942 they were flown in India on the eve of the fall of Rangoon,
and were carried at the Victory parade in Delhi in 1945.

In 1881, it was decided that all infantry regiments would have white colours. This would
have meant replacing the distinctive yellow of the 28th Regimental Colour. Rather than do
so, the 28th (in common with the 61st) contrived to retain their old Colour by zealously
repairing the torn and perished silk. In 1929, the King approved a return to the former
colours. By 1952 the old 28th Colours were too frail for further service and were replaced by
a new set, presented by HRH The Duke of Gloucester. The old colours were then laid up in
Gloucester Cathedral, where they hang to this day.

The King's Colour (left) and Regimental Colour of the 28th in Lucknow 1904. The piled drums of the regiment are emblazoned with the battle honours stitched on the regimental Colour. These same Colours were carried until 1953.

allowed to add to its Colours the names of earlier battles. Thus the earliest honour is that for Ramillies in 1706 when the 28th fought under the Duke of Marlborough. Most recent is 'Imjin' from the Korean War in 1951. At this battle, the 1st Battalion earned another unique distinction which is carried on the Regimental Colour: a blue silk streamer, which is the emblem of the US Presidential Citation for valour.

The number of honours earned by all regiments during the two World Wars was so great that there was no room to fit them on the Regimental Colours. Therefore ten honours from each war were selected, and placed on the King's Colour.

THE BAND AND DRUMS

An important feature of any regimental occasion is the regimental band, usually accompanied by the Corps of Drums. There has always been a strong connection between soldiers and music. Lively tunes played by the band and drums have, over the years, lightened the step of many a footsore soldier at the end of a day's march or served as a distraction from enemy cannon balls as he advanced into battle. During the battle, if they were not required to play, the band would act as stretcher bearers to recover the wounded. To this day, they play at regimental weddings, baptisms and church parades. When a soldier dies the drums are muffled and draped in black, and the band accompanies his funeral service. In the days before wireless and television the regimental music was the main source of entertainment

The 4th (City of Bristol) Battalion of the Glosters was converted to an artillery searchlight unit in 1940. In July 1944, the Colours were paraded through the streets of Bristol, badly blitzed in 1941, to be handed over to the Lord Mayor for safekeeping until the end of the war. Lieutenants Woodbridge and Larkman carried the Colours. The battalion was disbanded in October 1945.

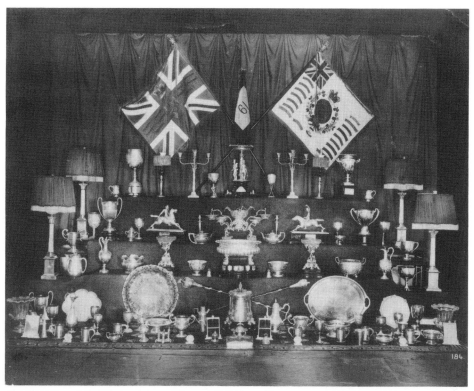

The Colours, and Officers' Mess Silver of the 61st – Jhansi, 1928. Most of the Glosters' silver is of recent origin. That of the 61st was largely destroyed in the Indian Mutiny when mutineers burnt down the Mess. The silver had been buried but was melted by the heat of the fire. Most of the silver of the 28th was lost during the retreat from Burma in 1942.

for the officers and men when they were off duty. Concert parties, in which the band played a prominent part, were the backbone of Christmas celebrations, especially overseas.

Whereas bandsmen are professional musicians, the drummers were, and remain, soldiers first and musicians second. In the early days, there were two drummers to each company. They often joined as boys and would be placed under the command of the drum major. Where the soldiers wore red jackets with yellow or buff facings, the colours on the coats of the drummers were reversed. They suffered many casualties as a result of this distinctive dress, which was abolished during the Napoleonic War. In later years they were to be distinguished by the 'drummers lace' on their red tunics, which is still worn today.

The drummers were the forerunners of today's radio operators for their task was to interpret orders and pass them on, initially by drum-beat but later in the nineteenth century, by bugle call. They acted as runners to deliver messages and, when required, had the unenviable task of carrying out floggings. Some would be trained in the fife, and it is recorded that the 28th marched off to Waterloo while the drums and fifes played 'The young May moon is shining love'.

The Band of the 28th at Aldershot in 1924.

The Corps of Drums, Jhansi, India, 1926. The long shadows tell us that these drummers of the 61st are parading in the cool of the day. The vultures in the thorn trees were a familiar feature of the Indian landscape.

The band and drums of the 3rd Battalion (Militia) relax before an engagement in 1892.

For regimental church services in the open air, the drums are piled to make an altar. Here a service is held for the Old Soldiers' Day at the depot in 1932.

Drummers would often join the army as boys, sometimes as young as 12 years old. Most were the sons of regular soldiers and were born within the regiment, which was their whole world.

The drum major is an imposing figure with his silver-topped mace and sash embroidered with regimental battle honours. Here in tropical dress is Drum Major P.R. Brown of the 28th in 1935, in Mhow, India. He enlisted as a drummer boy in 1919 aged 14. His performance in action would match up to his appearance. In 1940, during the battle at Cassel in France, he was awarded the Distinguished Conduct Medal for his gallantry in saving an officer's life.

REGIMENTAL CUSTOMS

Every regiment has its special customs and traditions which mark them apart from others, and the Glosters are no exception. Many of these customs are observed in the officers' messes of the regiment. The name 'mess' derives from an old French word for 'dish' or 'meal', and came to mean the place where men took their meals together. Apart from being a useful way for impecunious officers to share expenses, the act of dining together regularly helped to develop comradeship and 'esprit de corps' among the members of the Mess. The formalities associated with dining in the Mess also served to set standards of behaviour and dress, which were important for the maintenance of morale and example by the officers during a campaign. In primitive wartime conditions it is only too easy to let standards of discipline and cleanliness slip. When this happens, disease, low morale and disaster are not far off. However, it has always been a point of honour in the British Army that the officers should not dine until the needs of the men, animals and vehicles were attended to first.

So important for collective morale was the act of dining together considered to be that the regiment would go to extraordinary lengths to achieve it. A regimental dinner of the 28th was held during the Peninsular War in 1813 to celebrate the second anniversary of the battle of Albuhera on 16 May. As there were no chairs or tables available, a mess table, large enough to seat a hundred was dug out of the

The Officers' Mess – Wasirabad, 1855. Despite the heat, these officers of the 61st are clearly determined to maintain the Victorian dress code. Their facial whiskers are also characteristic of the time. Two years later, these officers were to lead the 61st during the Indian Mutiny.

Subalterns' parade, 1894. Young officers of the 61st parade in their mess kit, possibly for an adjutant's inspection. The adjutant was responsible for discipline and dress in his battalion and would have kept a sharp eye on the subalterns. They wear the first formal mess kit of the regiment worn between 1872 and 1895, a scarlet shell jacket with gold lace and braid.

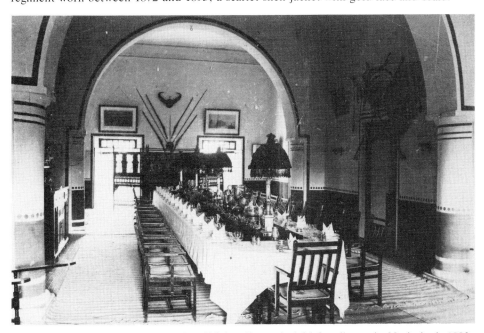

The table of the 61st Officers' Mess Dining Room is laid for dinner in Nasirabad, 1893. Surrounded by big game trophies and pictures, it would have been a comfortable place to dine in the company of one's brother officers. The silver columns on the table support oil lamps which, having been converted to electricity, are still in use today.

Sergeants' Mess ante room, Mustapha Pasha Barracks, Alexandria, Egypt, 1896. Simpler, but no less formal than the Officers' Mess, membership of the Warrant Officers' and Sergeants' Mess is the ambition of the long service regular soldier.

Despite the cheerful and informal camaraderie of these Volunteer officers from Gloucester at annual camp between 1900 and 1905, the maintenance of a good Mess in the field was as important as it was in barracks.

Combined Mess Dinner of the Officers of the 2nd, 4th, 5th, 6th Battalions and the depot at the Bristol Club, May 1938. The officers are wearing the distinctive scarlet mess jacket of the Glosters, worn from 1908 until the 1960s. It is based upon a traditional hunt design and is quite unlike that of any other regiment. The silk facings are primrose yellow.

turf. The turf was removed, a trench dug around the 'table' and the earth packed on top and levelled; the turf serving as the table cloth! On this and other such occasions, the culminating moment of the dinner would be the loyal toast to the health of the Sovereign.

Another notable dinner of the 28th was held after the battle of Barrosa, in March 1811. The normal custom for the loyal toast is for the president at the head of the table to rise and propose the toast 'Mr Vice – the Queen', whereupon the vice-president at the foot of the table rises to reply, 'Gentlemen – the Queen'. After Barossa, it happened that only two officers had survived the day's fighting. At the appropriate moment, the senior officer rose to propose the toast in the usual way, 'Mr Vice – The King'. At this, the other officer stood up and changed the reply to 'The King, Mr President!'. Officers of The Gloucestershire Regiment still celebrate the loyal toast in this unique way. Such eccentricities, which often mystify outsiders, contribute to the character and identity of a regiment and, *inter alia*, set it apart from others.

Chapter 4
SPORT AND LEISURE

Football has grown into a national pastime, in which the Army eagerly takes part; and the officers, not content with working with their men, have steadily played with them. In other armies such an association of all ranks on a common footing might be regarded as dangerous to discipline. In the British Army an officer who has led his men to victory in a football match will be the more devotedly followed by them in a sterner field.

Sir John Fortescue
The History of the British Army, vol XIII (1930)

In the first century of the regiment's existence, the idea that there should be organized sport or leisure activities for the soldiers would have been treated with scorn by officers and men alike. Most soldiers were too preoccupied with survival to think of recreation in any terms other than the oblivion induced by cheap liquor that helped them forget the brutal rigours of the life they led. Any other spare time was more likely to be spent in search of female company, firewood, or additional rations than in reading what the Victorians called 'improving literature'.

The image of a rapacious and licentious soldiery was still very strong in the early nineteenth century. Even Wellington, who had the greatest respect for the fighting qualities of his men and a real affection for them was wont to describe them as 'the scum of the earth'. Few people had a good word to say for the soldier, and perhaps it is not surprising that he tended to live up to, or rather down to, his public image.

Until mid-Victorian times, officers often delegated many of their duties and thus had more time to devote to sporting pursuits. Since many came from country estates, they would take every opportunity to go hunting, coursing or wildfowling. Each officer was responsible for maintaining his own horse. Fox hunting was regarded as excellent training for war, since it bred confidence and an eye for country. Packs of hounds were kept in Portugal during the Peninsular War and the officers would hunt the wolf, hare and wild boar during quiet periods. There is even record of a regimental race meeting in Portugal in 1810.[1]

ORGANIZED SPORTS

Despite the harsh life of the soldiers and the rigid class divisions of the time, years of campaigning had developed a spirit of mutual respect and comradeship between officer and men. It was in the Peninsula during the winter of 1812/13 that we see an early record of organized sports for the men. The regimental history records:

> We frequently got up foot-races . . . played matches at football, and rackets against the tower of the village church; had duck hunting with the dogs in a piece of water; and sometimes turned a pig loose with his tail greased, when he was pursued by the soldiers, and became the lawful prize of the man who could catch and hold him, which was no easy matter.[2]

As the nineteenth century progressed, the 28th and the 61st saw service in Ireland, India and Australia. With the expansion of Empire, the army settled down to its task of Imperial policing and the small wars which were a characteristic of Queen Victoria's reign. During this period, every type of sport flourished, encouraged by the Victorian enthusiasm for manliness and team spirit. For some, it was their first opportunity to play games. Football, for years a popular working-class game, had been largely forgotten by the civilian population where those in employment worked long hours, commonly from dawn to dusk six days a week. Not until the Saturday half-holiday became commonplace in the middle of the nineteenth century did working men have time for sports again.

TROPHY HUNTING

Victorian India swarmed with game of all sorts and both battalions served there at regular intervals from 1842 until eventual independence in 1947. For the officers, as well as shooting for the pot to eke out the men's meagre rations, trophy hunting was a popular diversion. The scrapbooks of the regiment include several pictures of the day's bag which ranged from wild duck, hare and grouse to the Himalayan

Members of the 61st look on as General Birdwood, Army Commander in Northern India, prepares to present the Muree Brewery Soccer cup to the battalion team in 1923. The tournament was open to all units stationed in Northern India, and had previously been won by the 61st in 1907. Such local successes whilst the battalion was stationed in Jhansi were greatly sought after.

A 61st tug of war team in the years before the First World War.

The Gloucestershire Rifle Volunteers, *c.* 1875. An interest in shooting attracted many recruits to the part-time Volunteers Corps. Locally raised units, such as this one from the Forest of Dean, were a spontaneous public response to fears of French invasion in 1859. The Volunteers were sanctioned by the Government provided there was no cost to the public. Apart from their rifles, everything else was supplied at private expense. They wore green uniforms with black leather accoutrements in the rifle tradition. In 1908, the Volunteers were incorporated into the forerunner of today's Territorial Army.

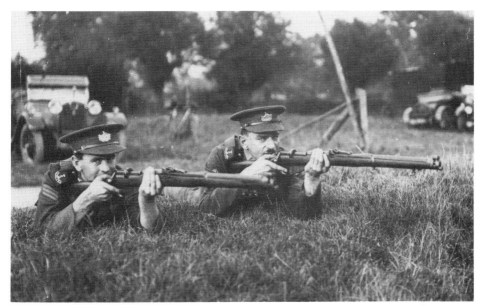

Riflemen of the 5th Territorial Battalion of the regiment shoot at Sneedham's Green Range, Gloucester in an annual competition between the regimental depot, the home service regular battalion and the 4th, 5th and 6th Territorial Battalions. Each man fired seven shots at 200, 500 and 600 yards. In 1930, when this photograph was taken, the 5th Battalion won the competition for the third successive year, a considerable feat.

This 45-pound mahseer, a fighting fish found in the rocky streams of Kashmir, was caught by an officer of the 61st while on leave from Jhansi, India in 1923.

Second-Lieutenant D.S. Strachan-Audas of the 28th, winner of the Central India Pig-Sticking Cup in 1935. Hunting wild pig, spear in hand on the back of a horse galloping through thick scrub over treacherous ground, was a dangerous sport. The pigs had razor-sharp tusks and, when cornered in close country, were formidable opponents.

brown bear, sambhur, ibex and tiger. Some officers took leave to fish in Kashmir where they did battle with the mighty mahseer in streams among the Himalayan foothills. Others painted, collected butterflies or experimented with the art of photography. Amateur dramatics and bridge parties were also popular.

INTER-UNIT COMPETITION

Team sports became better organized and competitions between regiments were encouraged. These maintained fitness, relieved the tedium of peacetime soldiering and kept the soldiers out of the grog shops. A silver model rowing boat in the Officers' Mess records the success of the 28th in Malta where they won the Governor's Cup twice in 1874 and 1894. Meanwhile the 61st gained distinction in India and Aden by winning the Infantry Polo Cup in 1893 and 1894. It was the custom of the 61st, when in India, to celebrate the anniversary of the battle of Chillianwallah with an athletics meeting, each January. A programme of the Chillianwallah Games held in India in 1856 includes such contests as Running in a Sack, Pony Race (loser to win), Old Soldiers' Race (16 years' service), Three Standing Leaps, and a Pig Hunt. When at home, such events were impractical in January and it was more convenient to commemorate the anniversary of Salamanca in July.

Recruits were taught to play games at the regimental depot on joining the army. Rugby was, and remains, particularly popular. Both battalions excelled at Rugby Football, first played in the army in 1855. Between them they won the Calcutta Cup

Officers of the 61st – winners of the Infantry polo trophy in India in 1893. Their shirts and the *pagri* band on their polo helmets are in the regimental colours. The sport of polo originated in Persia and was adopted by the British in India, where every garrison had its polo ground. The tournaments were great social occasions for all ranks and their families. All officers were expected to play and many maintained ponies at their own expense. The ponies would be schooled before breakfast and games played in the late cool of the day. Competitions were taken seriously and success was highly prized.

Malta 1894, the winning boat. A silver boat in the Officers' Mess commemorates the winning of the Governor's Cup by the 28th in 1874 and 1894. The cox is Lieutenant-Colonel G. Conner, who was stroke in the winning boat twenty years earlier.

The 28th Regiment Rugby Football Team, winners of the Aldershot Cup, 1925–26. Seated third from left is Captain M.A. James VC, MC, who won the Victoria Cross in the First World War. In the back row (fourth from left) is Second-Lieutenant J.P. Carne who was to be awarded the VC twenty-five years later in Korea.

In 1938, the 61st Rugby team, captained by Lieutenant P.C.S. Heidenstam, defeated the Welsh Guards by a score of 3–0 to become the army champions. The 61st had previously been champions in 1910. The match was won by a penalty goal kicked in the first five minutes by Lieutenant A.J.A. Arengo-Jones. Both he and Lieutenant Heidenstam rose to the rank of brigadier and each later became Colonel of the Regiment.

in India outright three times between 1907 and 1944.[3] The 61st also won the Army Rugby Cup in 1910 and 1938, a feat their post-war successors have tried hard to emulate without success, despite coming close on many occasions. Other sports included cricket, athletics, swimming and tennis.

Boxing has always been popular in the Glosters, and the fortunes of the various company and battalion boxing teams are followed with keen interest by all ranks. The 28th, for example, during a spell of seventeen years' foreign service, won the all-India army boxing for three years in a row between 1906 and 1908. In 1934, the 61st won the army boxing title, going on to beat the RAF in the inter-service championship.

OFF PARADE

Another occasion which brought officers and men together was the annual celebration of the anniversary of Alexandria. Every 21 March, wherever the 28th happened to be, they celebrated with a parade in the morning, followed by a carnival or sports in the afternoon in which all ranks and many families took part. The tradition is continued to this day by the 1st Battalion. The culminating event of the day is the Back Badge Ball, held by the Warrant Officers' and Sergeants' Mess, to which many officers are invited as guests. For that evening, as a mark of the special trust in which the senior NCOs of the regiment are held, the Colours are placed in their care. Until midnight, they are under the watchful eye of a specially

The 61st Sergeants' cricket team – South Africa, *c.* 1902–3.

59

Mixed doubles around 1900 – somewhere in India. Such clubs were the focus of social life in the garrisons throughout the subcontinent.

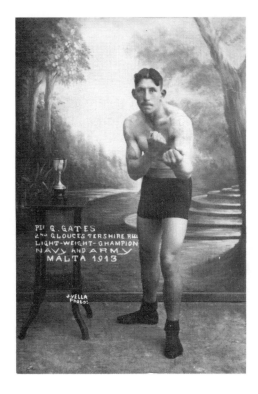

Both battalions of the regiment excelled at boxing. Private G. Gates was one of several inter-service boxing champions of the 61st during their tour in Malta between 1910 and 1913.

The Winning Team – 2nd Battalion, Jhansi, India. Central Provinces District Boxing Champions, 1924. The subaltern in the picture is Lieutenant C.E.A. Firth who later became a Major General, and was Colonel of the Regiment from 1954 to 1964.

During the inter-war years in India, much time was devoted to fitness training. Here the 61st Gymnastics team display their prowess and agility for the benefit of the camera. The photograph dates from 1925.

The Old Guard of the 28th Regiment, Lahore Ball, 1908.

Between the wars, the 6th Battalion took on a succession of Harlequin Great Danes as mascots. Each was taken on the strength and equipped with a coat in regimental colours for ceremonial occasions. On the left is Braggs III in 1938 with his handler, Sergeant Saunders. The regular battalions were less conventional, having at various times adopted a donkey, a brown bear and, in 1932, 'Bobby' a Shetland pony (right), mascot of the 28th in Singapore.

selected Old Guard, men dressed in uniforms of the Napoleonic period and allowed to grow their facial hair long for the occasion in the manner of 1801. At the stroke of midnight, the Old Guard are relieved by the New Guard, soldiers of today who guard the Colours until the ball is over.

As the nineteenth century drew to a close, life for the single soldier in barracks was a world away from the grim, squalid life of a hundred years before. Provided he could write, there was a reliable, if slow, mail service home. Although the NAAFI[4] did not yet exist, canteens were well established and monies honestly accounted for. Both the 28th and the 61st had regimental institutes which disbursed canteen profits and welfare funds to provide soldiers' comforts. They were supplemented by various charities, mostly temperance organizations, who would sell 'char and a wad'[5] for a few pence. By the time of the First World War, many of these organizations, such as the Salvation Army – known as the 'Sally Ann' – would run mobile canteens which followed the regiment wherever it served. They became familiar sights on manoeuvres, at the rifle range or behind the lines in war.

While overseas, single soldiers[6] often enjoyed a status that would have been impossible at home. In India in particular, he benefited from the services of the char[7] and dhobi-wallahs.[8] To the impoverished natives, a private soldier's wages represented unbelievable riches. Until the British Army left India in 1947, the soldier's routine domestic tasks could be carried out for him for a few pence. He could be shaved while he slept and awoken with a cup of tea to find his boots polished, equipment prepared, and his uniform pressed and starched alongside him. The contrast between this life and the frugal conditions at home could not have been more marked.

The 16 Platoon mule decked out with its Lewis Gun Harness, in the care of Private Workman. The scene is Mhow Gymkhana, India, 1932.

At home or overseas, soldiers now had more spare time and, apart from sport, had a chance to develop their hobbies. Shooting and fishing were no longer the exclusive preserve of the officers. Some soldiers raised vegetables or adopted stray animals and kept them as pets and mascots. Others used their time in search of simpler pleasures. RSM Pearce describes his time with the 28th in Cologne in 1923:

> Life was great in Germany as the mark had collapsed and I, as a Sergeant, was drawing, I think, about 6 million Marks. We drank champagne like water and the nightlife was terrific.[9]

As Rudyard Kipling once put it, in his poem devoted to Tommy Atkins:

> We aren't no thin red 'eroes, nor we aren't no blackguards too,
> But single men in barricks, most remarkable like you;
> An' if sometimes our conduck isn't all your fancy paints,
> Why, single men in barricks don't grow into plaster saints.

Chapter 5

THE FAMILIES

A woman when she marries a soldier ought to recollect that his profession entails on her definite and often very arduous duty . . . she has to bear as best she may the privations peculiar to her lot.

Honoria Lawrence,
wife of General Sir Henry Lawrence (1842)

Soldiers' wives are a special breed, they have to be – to put up with soldiers.

Army Padre (1980)[1]

The story of the Glosters would be incomplete without a mention of the women in their lives. Armies, whether on the march or in camp, in peace and in war, have always attracted hangers-on in their wake. Many of these camp followers were women who provided the soldier with a few physical and domestic comforts either free or for cash, as wives, prostitutes or tradeswomen. For two centuries, the presence of these women was grudgingly tolerated and acknowledged by the authorities. Not until the nineteenth century was the soldier's family fully recognized and its lot improved.

THE EARLY YEARS

In the early years of the regiment's history, married men were not allowed to enlist. Soldiers were discouraged from marrying and had to seek permission from their officers before doing so, although many defied the system. It was a hard life for the women who joined them. Home was wherever the regiment rested for the night, often a rough bivouac by an open fire. For the lucky ones there might be a corner of a barn or, if they could be afforded, lodgings at an inn. Since a soldier's pay was barely adequate for his own needs, let alone those of dependents, extra pennies had to be earned. The women would take in laundry, cook rations and mend other soldiers' or officers' linen.

In action, they would help to bring up ammunition, recover casualties and tend the wounded. If their men failed to return after a battle, they had to scour the battlefield with only a remote chance of finding them alive. If a woman's husband or lover died or abandoned her, she had to fend for herself. As widows overseas, they faced the daunting prospect of making their way back to England without assistance. Those who could not find a new protector were often faced with a choice between prostitution or destitution.

It was not until the 1790s that wives were officially recognized for the first time. Each 100-man company was allowed six women, 'legally' married to soldiers, to be taken 'on the strength'. If the regiment was fortunate and based in one of the new barracks built to house the rapidly expanding army of the Napoleonic War, these women were entitled to set up home in a corner of their husband's barrack room. 'Home' was a bedspace with a blanket or piece of sacking slung over a rope to give them some privacy from the thirty or so soldiers who shared the same room. In these primitive, and often unhealthy, conditions, children were conceived, born and raised, often to follow in their parents' footsteps for want of knowing a different life.

The families who survived developed tough constitutions. They travelled far and wide alongside their menfolk, sharing their hardships. They endured the foul conditions and perils of long sea voyages on postings abroad. On arrival they coped as best they could with the difficulties of living and rearing their children in a harsh and foreign land. Often they found themselves as spectators to great events. As the 28th were rowed, under fire, towards the French-held beaches in Egypt in 1801, the families lined the bulwarks of the transport ships listening to the gunfire and watching the confusion of battle. Once ashore, some would ride on one of the wagons of the baggage train or, more often, would travel on foot.

'ON THE STRENGTH'

Whilst 'on the strength', the wives were subject to military discipline. They could be flogged – and were – for drunkenness, brawling or dishonest trading.[2] On route marches, they and their children had to keep up with their men for their own safety. To be left behind meant abandonment, starvation, exposure or death at the hands of a hostile population or enemy troops.

The experiences of Mary Grant, an Irish girl who married Thomas McClelland of the 28th in 1803, are not uncommon. Her father made his son-in-law promise that he would not take his new bride into barracks until she was 'older, and more used to the service'. Thus they lived in lodgings until the birth of their first child in 1805. They then sailed to Germany with the regiment and marched to Bremen. After a brief return to England in 1807 when another child was born, they went back to the Continent during the campaign to capture the Danish Fleet at Copenhagen. Returning to England in 1808, they endured another sea journey to Sweden, where they were not allowed to land, and were then diverted to Portugal to join General Moore's army. During the terrible retreat to Corunna, both Mary's children died. In 1810 she and her husband were sent with the 28th to Southern Spain but, shortly afterwards, Sergeant McClelland was killed at the battle of Barrosa. Mary then married one of her husband's friends, Sergeant Ball,[3] and accompanied him, throughout the Peninsular campaign, from Gibraltar to the Pyrenees. She bore him several children, of whom two joined the army.

Although discouraged from early marriage, on the grounds that their first duty was to their men, young officers had more freedom to marry than soldiers. Expected to possess private incomes, officers were also better able to care for their spouses. As opposed to soldiers' 'women' or sergeants' 'wives', officers' 'ladies', therefore, could follow their husbands in relative comfort, either on horseback or in a carriage with servants to attend to their domestic needs. Nevertheless, the perils faced on the march by the officers' wives were no less severe than those to which the soldiers and their wives were subjected.

THE PERILS OF PEACETIME

'Peace' is sometimes defined as 'the absence of war', but for those 'following the drum', life could still be hazardous and uncomfortable, particularly in the new colonies of North America, India and Australia. Privation, disease and local insurrections claimed the lives of many women and children whenever they accompanied soldiers. In 1843 during the Indian Sikh Wars, the 28th lost 350 men out of 1,000 and most of their women and children through cholera, dysentery or heat exhaustion.

In 1845, the 61st and their families sailed for India from Ireland in five ships. Two weeks out of port, they ran into a storm and one ship lost two masts. Babies were born and six men died of typhus in what was described as an 'uneventful' voyage. They landed in Calcutta 126 days later, and travelled the 600 miles to Cawnpore by river. Six months later, to reach their final destination of Amballa, the women and children had to cover the remaining 394 miles on foot. The journey took thirty-four days in oppressive heat, while the nights were sometimes enlivened by brigand attacks. Once, when the regiment was ordered to pack up the tents, an officer asked if he could keep his up since his wife had been robbed during the night and was left with nothing but a straw hat and a crinoline.[4] Fourteen years later, having lived through the terror of the Indian Mutiny, the 61st and their families left Delhi on a ninety-three-day march to Bombay, *en route* to Mauritius.

POST-CRIMEAN REFORM

When the 28th set off for the Crimean War in 1854, it was to be the last time that wives and children were allowed to accompany their husbands on active service. As descriptions of the living conditions of soldiers and families appeared in the British press, the full horror shocked the public at home. Military reform followed, reflecting changes in social attitudes which were occurring throughout Victorian England. A programme of barrack building was begun, including, for the first time, permanent quarters for married men and their families. The pioneering work of Florence Nightingale led to the establishment of proper medical care for wounded soldiers. The design of a portable camp stove by Monsieur Soyer, a celebrated French chef, was but the first step along a road which led eventually to organized regimental kitchens. Although designed to improve the lot of the soldier, the reforms had the added effect of reducing the burden on soldiers' wives, who had traditionally carried out many of these tasks.

By the beginning of the First World War, permanent garrisons, with their distinctive style of architecture, had been established all over Britain and overseas. Large accommodation blocks with sweeping verandahs often included separate wings for married families.[5] Others were housed in terraces of 'two up, two down' houses, while more imposing terraces or detached villas were made available for

The distinctive shape of this Victorian colonial barrack block and stables included the married quarters in Mustapha Pasha Barracks, Alexandria, photographed in 1896.

A part-time territorial soldier of the Glosters poses with his wife and children, possibly on the eve of mobilization for the Great War when such pictures were common. On his sleeve, the reversed chevrons each indicate one year of exemplary military conduct. The TA was originally raised to defend the UK but from 1912, individuals could volunteer to serve overseas. The metal 'Imperial Service' badge is above the soldier's right pocket.

James and John Day were twins who served together in the Glosters in the 1930s. The tradition of family service is well established in the regiment.

A regimental butcher unloads beef from the back of a truck during battalion training of the 7th Battalion in December 1939. In the background, a fatigueman is tending a Soyer Stove, first introduced for Crimean service in 1842 and still in use today.

officers' families. In sharp contrast to earlier times, when privacy was at a premium, unit standing orders would make it clear that married quarters were reserved for married people. Except on duty, such as delivering coal or removing dustbins, single men were excluded. To visit friends a special pass was required.

Despite these welcome improvements, many quarters were rudimentary, furnished only with the bare essentials. Whenever families moved with the regiment their baggage was restricted to clothing and a few knick-knacks. Beds, tables, chairs, cupboards and a tin bath were provided, but not much else. The basic nature of married quarters would remain unchanged for many years. When he returned to Gravesend from India in 1929, Company Sergeant-Major Pearce's family was housed in a converted barrack room.

> The walls were not even plastered. Heating and cooking was by means of an open range. We had a fuel ration and were issued with rations: 1lb of meat every day – issued in two joints of 3 or 4 lbs – a loaf of bread every two days . . . tea and sugar at the end of each month and an allowance of 1 shilling per day paid out at the end of each month.[6]

In 1935, the army decided to start 'At Homes' in order to show civilians something of the life led by soldiers and their families. In Bristol, the gates were thrown open at Horfield Barracks, and 7,000 visitors passed through to see what lay behind the forbidding grey walls of the regimental depot. Here, young soldiers of the regiment, dressed in period uniforms of the 28th and 61st, are selling programmes and extolling the virtues of military service to some potential recruits.

The allowance was meant to compensate him for the loss of free food which he would have received in the regimental cookhouse as a single soldier.

LIFE ABROAD

From the late nineteenth century onwards, life abroad was more comfortable for the families than at home. Many soldiers' wives experienced for the first time the luxury of domestic help. There was much social activity to compensate for the lack of public entertainment. Within the narrow confines of the imperial cantonments, families created their own amusements, ranging from race meetings and concert parties to picnics and charity bazaars. While such activities were often determined by the rank and status of the husband they were, nonetheless, more relaxed and exciting than many a wife would have experienced back home. It was in the outposts of the Empire that the regimental family, as a self sufficient social unit, came into its own. Far away from home, and in unfamiliar surroundings, strong

The wedding in Ceylon of Captain John Ingram of the 28th, *c.* 1900. Weddings overseas made few concessions to the climate and followed the traditional English pattern. The 28th had been separated from their families by the war in South Africa between 1899–1900. Afterwards the 28th were sent to Ceylon to guard Boer prisoners of war. Captain Ingram had been a prisoner of the Boers himself for a while, and his bride was no doubt relieved to see him. He was to serve for a further twenty years and survived the Great War, where he won the Distinguished Service Order.

Major Archdale and Lieutenant Burges of the 61st (in bow ties) enjoy a rural picnic with their friends in Rajputana, *c.* 1892. The native bearers would have seen to the arrangements for food and refreshments.

Every summer in India, those who could do so headed for the foothills of the Himalayas to escape from the heat of the plains. Darjeeling was the favourite hill station for those based in the Calcutta area. The curved track of the famous mountain railway wound its way slowly up the steep gradients, the air growing fresher and cooler with every mile that passed.

The spacious bungalows in Jalapahar were home for British officers' families and their servants from April to October. Between 1815 and 1947, the British created over eighty such hill stations. Husbands would get away to join their families whenever duty allowed, usually taking up to eight weeks' leave. For the rest of the time, their wives became 'grass widows'.

The province of Kashmir was a favourite sporting and holiday destination in British India. Srinagar, with its lakes and houseboats, was a popular and much photographed honeymoon spot. The photograph dates from 1920.

Sergeant H.W. Whittern's wedding reception at Major Dinham's bungalow, Rawalpindi, between 1920 and 1923. Rawalpindi in Northern India was described as a station of 'continual heat, guards and duties'. Sergeant Whittern was decorated with the Military Medal for his gallantry during the First World War. Major E.H. Dinham (seated fourth from left) commanded B Company and it is likely that Whittern served under him. Major Dinham joined the Regiment as a soldier in 1888, fought with the 61st throughout the Boer and First World Wars, and was commissioned in 1904 as Quartermaster. As a former member of the Sergeants' Mess, he would not have hesitated to offer Whittern the facilities of his bungalow for the wedding celebrations.

Families of the 28th at a Sports Day in Cairo between the wars. The absence of menfolk and the uniformity of the sun hats suggests that the photo may have been taken at a local school for British children. Free education for the children of married soldiers was an important benefit, at home and abroad. In 1920, there were 190 army schools, most of them overseas, including thirteen in Egypt.

In February 1950, shortly after the 28th/61st returned from Jamaica, they were visited in Colchester by their Colonel-in-Chief, HRH The Duke of Gloucester. He is seen here with the Commanding Officer, Lieutenant Colonel J.P. Carne, meeting selected ladies of the regiment. The local milliner appears to have done a roaring trade! Eight months later the battalion embarked for Korea, leaving the soldiers' families behind in Colchester.

2nd Battalion children at a fancy dress party in Malta, 1910. Nurses' uniforms for the girls and officers' mess kits for the boys are in keeping with the patriotic fervour of the early twentieth century.

bonds developed between the women who had married into regiments such as the Glosters. Irrespective of rank, in emergencies, on high days and holidays, everyone joined in or pulled together.

At the outbreak of the Second World War, the families found themselves in Burma with the 28th, having arrived there from India with the battalion in 1938. When Japan entered the war in December 1941, the battalion was mobilized. At first, attempts by the commanding officer to evacuate the families had been denied on the grounds that it was 'unnecessary and bad for morale'. As Rangoon was bombed and the Japanese threat became immediate, they were given forty-eight hours' notice in which to pack, taking with them only what they could carry. Some were reluctant to leave but soon appreciated the necessity, notwithstanding the formation of 'The 28th Ladies Rifle Club' as a mark of resistance. On Christmas Day 1941, Japanese bombs fell on the married quarters. Fortunately, most of the families had already left on a long journey which took them by rail, plane, river launch and foot to Northern Burma, and thence to India. Eventually they arrived in Calcutta, but it was months before the husbands heard that their families had reached safety. It was just as long before the families received any news of their husbands. The families of Glosters captured in France in 1940 and later in Korea endured similar periods of uncertainty.

Soldiers' wives are sometimes patronized by those who use such expressions as 'they also serve who only stand and wait'. Yet they have always been resourceful and the Glosters' wives played as active a part in the life of the regiment as any. Frequently separated from their menfolk by war or the demands of the service, the regimental wives have kept the home fires burning, reared their children, and coped with a host of minor and major emergencies which those with husbands in less demanding professions rarely encounter. Over time, they developed as fierce a

Private Mustoe and his family (seated at the front above the middle window) with other members of the 1st Battalion on a pleasure cruise from Cologne to Koblenz c. 1922. The battalion spent a year in Germany serving with the occupying troops of the Army of the Rhine.

loyalty to each other and the regiment as any serving member and wore with pride their sweetheart brooches in the shape of the regimental badge. That pride continues today in the hearts of Mary Grant's successors:

We are a tough lot. We have had to be. For more than 300 years we have travelled the world with our men, often at a moment's notice. We have loved and courted, married and bore children in all parts of the globe. Our ghosts must surely haunt married quarters up and down the British Isles, in Gibraltar, Malta, Bermuda, Germany and the Curragh. We kept house in Bungalows in India, Malaya, Hong Kong, Shanghai and the West Indies and in the dwellings of South Africa, North America and Canada. We endured capture, wounding, imprisonment, kidnapping, shipwreck, rape and murder.[7]

Chapter 6
KEEPING THE PEACE: SERVICE AT HOME AND ABROAD

My name is O'Kelly, I've heard the Revelly
From Birr to Bareilly, from Leeds to Lahore,
Hong Kong and Peshawur,
Lucknow and Etawah,
And fifty-five more all endin' in 'pore'.

Rudyard Kipling
Shillin' a Day

During the late nineteenth century, as the photographers' art began to blossom, the British Army, including the Glosters, was largely stationed overseas in the various garrisons set up to protect British interests.

THE EMERALD ISLE

Closest to home was the large garrison maintained in Ireland where both the 28th and the 61st spent much time. In 1865, there were over 600 Irishmen serving in the 61st. Between 1720 and 1992, the regiment served over seventy years in the Emerald Isle. The first tour lasted twenty-three years! A reminder of this long association is the regimental march, a cheerful Irish jig called *The Kinnegad Slashers*.[1] The troubled history of Ireland is a familiar subject today but, apart from recent years, much of the time spent there by the Glosters was comparatively tranquil. Difficult times were rare, such as the violent period between 1920 and partition in 1922 when the old 28th was sent to keep the peace in County Cork.

LIFE IN INDIA

'Keeping the Peace' has been a familiar if somewhat contradictory feature of peacetime service for the Glosters. From the mid-nineteenth century onwards, the priority for the army was to protect British commercial and trading interests by the active defence of British colonial possessions. The crown jewel of the Empire, and the focus of Imperial policing, was India. The first of many tours for the Glosters in the subcontinent began in 1842, when the 28th was despatched to Bombay after

A Rolls Royce armoured car edges gingerly over a makeshift bridge to cross a culvert destroyed by the IRA in 1921. Members of the 28th look on.

Lorries were armoured in Ireland during the 1920s to give protection against IRA ambush, and were forced to travel in convoys. The restricted visibility for their drivers made them difficult vehicles to manoeuvre on narrow country roads.

Surgeon H.T. Reade of the 61st was awarded the VC for his actions during the assault on Delhi in the Indian Mutiny in 1857. He was tending the wounded when they came under fire. Drawing his sword, he gathered some soldiers around him and dislodged the mutineers under heavy fire. Two days later, he was in the forefront of the regiment's assault on the Delhi magazine, once again showing great gallantry. His VC, the first awarded to the regiment, is now in the Regimental Museum in Gloucester. Surgeon Reade was born in Canada and later went on to become Surgeon General to the army.

A detachment of the 1st Battalion at the Royal Tournament in 1931, dressed as members of the 61st, in examples of the home-dyed khaki uniforms which the regiment first adopted at Delhi. They are re-enacting Surgeon Reade's winning of the VC and are carrying the Enfield muzzle-loading rifles which had replaced the Brown Bess in 1857. At the time, many soldiers were suspicious of the new rifle and preferred the more familiar musket when fighting the mutineers.

seven years spent guarding the convict settlements in Australia. Within nine months, 232 officers, men, wives and children of the Regiment had died of cholera. By the time the 28th returned home in 1848, there were few survivors from the battalion which had left England thirteen years before. Its strength had been maintained only by a succession of drafts of new recruits from Gloucestershire and Bristol.

The 61st sailed from Ireland to India in 1845 and remained overseas for fourteen years, thirteen of them in India. They had fought in the Second Sikh War and in the Indian Mutiny. During the Mutiny, the 61st was part of the force which recaptured Delhi from the mutineers.

AWARDS FOR GALLANTRY

During the bitter fighting in the narrow streets of Delhi, Surgeon Reade of the 61st became one of the first to be awarded the newly instituted Victoria Cross for his gallantry in the forefront of the action against the enemy. Such gallantry awards were rare, but it now became commonplace for soldiers to be awarded medals for campaign service. A bar would be attached to the ribbon of the medal showing the names of each of the major battles in which the recipient had fought.

Within a year of the end of the Napoleonic War, all ranks who had fought at Waterloo had been awarded the Waterloo Medal. This was a significant departure from earlier practice when the only medals given usually went to commanding officers. Eventually, thirty-four years after the war finished, a medal was also given

Taken in Devonport in 1861 after the 61st returned from India following the siege of Delhi, the picture shows officers wearing all the different forms of dress current at the time. Surgeon H.T. Reade VC is seated second from the left.

A late nineteenth-century view of the Gate of the Old Magazine where much bitter fighting took place during the assault on Delhi. Surgeon Reade earned his VC not far from here. The gate still exists.

to all those who fought in the Peninsular War. It included a bar for 'Egypt' awarded to the 28th, a rarity much prized by medal collectors. Now, in the 1850s, there were new medals with bars inscribed 'Goojerat', 'Chillianwallah', 'Punjab', 'Alma', 'Inkerman', 'Sevastopol' and 'Delhi 1857'.

THE LONG PEACE

With the Crimea and the Mutiny behind it, a long period of peace followed for the regiment. The 61st left India in 1859 and served in Mauritius, Canada, Ireland, Malta and the Channel Islands before returning to India again in 1880. During the same period the 28th, which arrived in India just too late to help put down the Mutiny, was stationed in Malta, Hong Kong, Singapore and Gibraltar.

The formal linkage of the 28th and 61st in 1881 as the 1st and 2nd Battalions of The Gloucestershire Regiment saw the establishment of a regimental depot in Bristol at Horfield. Here, recruits to the regiment would receive between sixteen and eighteen weeks' basic training in drill, fieldcraft and musketry before being sent to one of the battalions. The depot was to remain at Horfield until 1940, when it moved to Reservoir Camp in Gloucester.[2]

Also affected by the 1881 reorganization were the local militia and corps of

John Sloman joined the 61st in India in 1854, and took part in the assault on Delhi, where his commanding officer remarked upon his gallantry. He retired in about 1873.

In the nineteenth century, the senior non-commissioned officer in a regiment was appointed as Sergeant Major. Competition was fierce and only the best of soldiers could aspire to this exalted position. Sergeant Major Baker was a remarkable man who enlisted in 1842 and was present at the battle of Chillianwallah. During the assault on Delhi he captured the colours of the 41st Native Infantry. In recognition of his bravery he was offered a commission but turned it down for family reasons, and was awarded the Distinguished Conduct Medal. He retired in 1863 and later became a yeoman warder at the Tower of London. To this day the Regimental Sergeant Major of the 1st Battalion carries Sergeant Major Baker's cane. He died in 1910 aged 84. His son also became RSM and a yeoman warder. For over a century there have been Bakers serving in the regiment.

volunteers, who were the forerunners of today's Territorial Army. The Militia was a well-established organization of part-time soldiers who were embodied in time of war. In 1881 the South and North Gloucester Militia became the 3rd and 4th Battalions of the regiment.

The Volunteers were an additional reserve who were only raised in times of national emergency to supplement the Militia and the regular army. The 1st and 2nd Battalions of the Gloucestershire Rifle Volunteers were formed in 1859. Their uniforms, drill halls and rifle ranges depended upon the generosity of local landowners or public subscription. Under these circumstances it is not surprising that uniforms were somewhat fanciful and social activities tended to take priority over military manoeuvres. It is said that for ceremonial parades, the Militia in Bristol would borrow the local tradesmen's horses. One commanding officer is alleged to have always been mounted on the horse which normally pulled the baker's van. As a result, nothing would make the horse move when the colonel ordered 'Quick March', unless a drummer boy was stationed close by to say 'No bread today, thank you, baker', after which the horse moved off![3] Nonetheless, enthusiasm was high and the volunteer ethos which developed in these early days was to provide a strong foundation when the time came to expand the army in the Boer War and two World Wars.

Neither regular battalion of the regiment had much opportunity to celebrate the closer link with Gloucestershire for, in 1881, both were far away; the 1st Battalion in Ireland and the 2nd in Baluchistan. In the years that followed, a new pattern of service developed with one battalion overseas and the other at home. The role of

Horfield Barracks, depot for the regiment from 1882 until 1942. The barracks also housed a regular artillery battery, to whom the gun in the background belonged. This scene of Changing the Guard dates from July 1938.

the home service battalion was to provide drafts of reinforcements to keep the foreign service battalion up to strength; in those days it was around 900 men. Apart from wartime, this pattern continued until the two battalions were amalgamated in 1948 in Jamaica.

During the long peace, both battalions in turn got to know the garrisons of England and Ireland. A list of their stations is a litany of towns familiar with the tramp of soldiers' feet; Portsmouth, York, Dublin, Plymouth and, of course, Aldershot. When their turn came for overseas service they and their families set up home in the cantonments of the Empire; in Karachi and Jhansi, Lucknow and Lahore, Bombay, Poona, Calcutta, Mhow and Madras. The opening of the Suez Canal in 1869 gave a new importance to the Eastern trade routes. Once again, the regiment found itself in Malta, Egypt, Aden, Ceylon or Singapore. One or other battalions of the regiment was based in Malta on seven separate occasions between 1854 and 1910. Several of the photographs in this book reflect life in this congenial Mediterranean outpost of Empire.

THE ORIENT

Twice the 2nd Battalion found itself in China protecting British trading interests. In 1913 it moved from Malta to Tientsin in North China. Hardly had the battalion arrived when the Great War broke out, and it was hurried home and sent to Flanders. In 1927 it was suddenly mobilized from Jhansi in India for what a later generation of Glosters would call an emergency tour. At that time the Chinese Civil

The 61st practise manoeuvres with live ammunition near Nasirabad in 1891. The sergeants (wearing sashes) are in the positions they would occupy in battle, where it was their duty to steady the ranks and prevent any soldier leaving without permission.

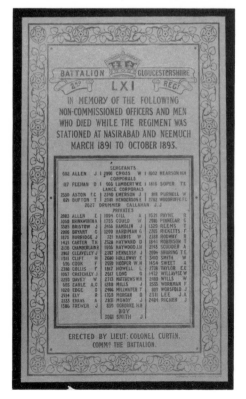

Soldiers serving overseas in Victorian times faced many dangers including disease. After the two-and-a-half years the 61st spent in Nasirabad, sixty-eight Glosters remained behind, their passing commemorated on this brass plaque erected in the garrison church.

War was at its height and there were fears for the safety of Europeans in the International Settlement in the port of Shanghai. From February to July 1927, the battalion 'showed the flag' to discourage warring Chinese factions from over-running the city. There was much civil disturbance and bitterness coupled with political complexities which did not make it an easy task to keep the peace. Fortunately the tension eased and the 61st was able to return to Jhansi.

ROUTINE OVERSEAS

Back in India, as in similar stations elsewhere in the subcontinent, the battalion settled into the routine of cantonment life, common to service overseas in the period between the wars. To avoid the heat of the midday sun, a typical day would begin with reveille at 4.30 a.m., breakfast at 4.45 a.m. and company parade at 5.30 a.m. Much of the training would take place before the sun reached its height. In the afternoon soldiers would often be left to their own devices, to see the sights or rest. Rest periods were commonly referred to as '*charpoy* bashing'[4] or, rather unkindly, 'Egyptian PT', the latter expression still in occasional use today. With the cool of the evening came organized sports and competitions. Great store was

Lieutenant Dickie Jordan sits at ease, beside his tent during a training camp of the 28th in Phoenix Park, Dublin, in 1891. His personal bath tub and the simple furnishings inside the tent would have been provided at his own expense. Having fought in the Boer War, he was to distinguish himself in command of the 7th Battalion at Gallipoli in 1915, where every officer and senior NCO was either killed or wounded within two hours.

Off-duty Glosters of the 28th stationed in Egypt in the 1920s were required to walk out in uniform. The sphinx and the pyramids at Gizeh (above) were popular tourist spots and who could resist a ride on a camel? Many such snaps, taken by the soldiers themselves, were sent home by the penny post for the family albums.

The Officers' Mess staff devour the pages of the *Thompsons Weekly* in Egypt, 1929. Mail and papers from home arrived regularly but were several weeks old by the time they reached the battalion.

Men of the 61st after a snowball fight in Tientsin, China, 1913. Soon they will be on their way back to Europe and the Great War.

The Drums of the 61st lead the way up the main street in Shanghai shortly after the Battalion disembarked in 1927 for peacekeeping duties.

A barricade manned by the 61st on the North Szechuan Road monitors traffic in the International Settlement, Shanghai, 1927.

Whilst on the march, the regiment covered fifteen or more miles a day, starting early in the morning cool, after a light breakfast. At various milestones along well-used routes, banyan trees were planted to provide shade during halts. Here officers of the 61st await their mid-morning meal (known in India as 'Tiffin'), which will be served by the bearers who stand in the background. The scene is the fifth milestone on the road to Ajmere, near Nasirabad, 1893.

A group of NCOs of the 28th with their company commander in Cairo, where the battalion was stationed from 1928 to 1931. The captain (centre) wears the Military Cross, awarded for gallantry. He is flanked by his company sergeant major (left) and company quartermaster sergeant (right). All are veterans of the First World War.

placed upon physical fitness and inter-platoon sixteen-mile runs were not uncommon.

TROOPSHIPS

When the time came for the battalion to go home, it would travel by troopship on a voyage lasting several weeks. In bad weather, conditions were often squalid and, for years afterwards, men would recall the stench of the crowded troop decks. Good days were more enjoyable when soldiers and their families could admire the flying fish, enjoy the sunshine or play Crown and Anchor, the only form of gambling that was permitted. They probably savoured every moment since the prospect of peacetime garrison soldiering in England held few attractions.

When the regiment returned home, it found an army which was undermanned (the foreign service battalions having the priority for manpower), underpaid[5] and poorly equipped. Promotion was by vacancy and was very slow. When young Philip Heidenstam joined the 61st from Sandhurst in 1934, the second in command of his company was Captain Manley James. James had won the VC in 1917, but was still only a captain some seventeen years later. It is small wonder that service overseas,

The lateen sails on the native dhows were a familiar sight to servicemen and their families aboard troopships in Bombay harbour in the late nineteenth century.

These massive marble arches mark the Gateway to India, the spot where passengers disembarked in Bombay, which took over from Calcutta as the principal point of entry to India after the opening of the Suez Canal in 1869.

On Guard – Egypt 1936
This picture of a soldier of the 61st was probably posed for public relations purposes during the regiment's emergency tour on the border with Libya.

Vickers machine-gun crew practise under simulated gas attack conditions – Egypt 1936.

A member of the 61st loses no opportunity to produce a mug of char on his primus stove, among the defences along the Libyan border, in 1936.

Wellington lies 6,000 ft up in the Nilgiri Hills in Southern India. After a year in the heat of Madras, the cooler climate provided a welcome relief for the 28th between 1937 and 1938. The surrounding countryside visible in this landscape is covered by jungle, eucalyptus and scrub. The barracks of the 28th lie in the centre. The nearest British unit was 200 miles away,

The battalion command car – Egypt, 1936.

so social life and opportunities for competitive sport were limited but whist drives, tombolas, dances and roller-skating were held by way of amusement in the evenings. The Nilgiris are the setting for Kipling's *Jungle Book* stories.

The funeral of Private Hill in Wellington, India, 1937. The drums (above) are draped with black as they lead the regimental funeral cortège towards the garrison cemetery. Soldiers rest on their arms reversed (below) as a mark of respect to their dead comrade, as his coffin passes by with an escort from the 28th.

where living was cheap and soldiering more fun, was sought after. Many then (and now) would echo the words of Rudyard Kipling:

> Ship me somewheres east of Suez, where the best is like the worst,
> Where there aren't no Ten Commandments an' a man can raise a thirst;
> For the temple-bells are callin' an' it's there that I would be –
> By the old Moulmein Pagoda, looking lazy at the sea;
> On the road to Mandalay . . .

In 1936, the 61st faced another quick move when, as a result of strained relationships with Italy over Mussolini's adventures in Africa, it was sent to Egypt for a year. Despite tedious guard duties on the frontier with Libya, the battalion still found time to play games and win the Command Rugby Cup. Some soldiers managed to visit the site of the memorial statue at Alexandria, erected in honour of Sir Ralph Abercromby, the army commander who was fatally wounded at the great battle where their forebears had fought so many years before.

Meanwhile, it had been the turn of the 28th as foreign service battalion. It left England in 1928 and after three years in Egypt, near Cairo, went to Singapore for a year, followed by eleven years in India. In 1938, it moved to Mingaladon near Rangoon, in Burma, and was still there when the Second World War broke out in 1939. It would be some time before the soldiers came home for, in December 1941, Japan entered the war.

Chapter 7

WAR

There is nothing certain about war – except that one side won't win.

Sir Ian Hamilton
Gallipoli Diary (1920)

Long ago, a popular toast among young officers in their cups was to a sudden plague or a quick war. With the optimism that only youth knows they meant that their senior officers should be the victims so that promotion and glory might fall to their juniors. Today, with the intensity and horrors of modern war displayed on television screens, that perspective seems naïve, even callous and obscene. Yet such views must be seen in the context of their time.

Until the nineteenth century it was possible to view warfare in a romantic light with gentlemanly rules of conduct. It was not that war was any less brutal then, rather that it was not portrayed as such. Apart from those with personal experience of the carnage at, say, Waterloo, others were dependent upon second hand accounts and folklore. Many were written by survivors who were either distant from the action or who sought to justify their own performance. Not until the first professional war correspondents appeared, such as W.H. Russell at the Crimea, did the general public gain any real understanding of what war was like. Even then, words without pictures conveyed varying images in the mind of the reader. Those who wished to cloud their perspective in a mist of patriotic fervour had little difficulty in doing so. Only with the advent of battlefield photography was this dewy-eyed notion of romantic adventurism finally dispelled.

THE BOER WAR: 1899–1902

Given the attitudes of the time, it is not surprising that the Boer War was described as the last of the Gentlemen's Wars. This was largely due to the observance of courtesies towards the wounded and lack of general personal enmity on both sides. In truth, there was little gentlemanly about a war which saw the widespread use of modern, accurate, long-range weapons and the introduction of concentration camps for civilian internees.

Both regular battalions of the regiment served in South Africa, in their first action for nearly fifty years. For the 28th in particular, it was a frustrating experience. Their commanding officer was killed in their first battle and the

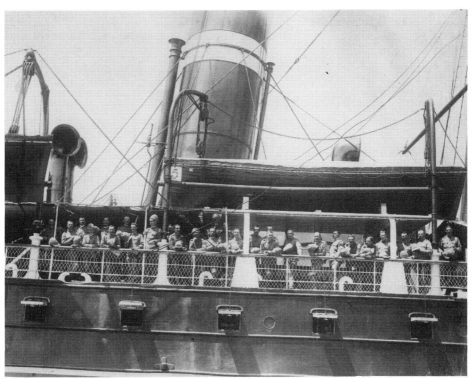

Officers of the 28th line the rails of the SS *India* in October 1899 as they prepare to sail for South Africa.

Officers of the 28th outside Ladysmith enjoy a brief respite before the privations of the siege, which would last for 120 days.

Picquets were small outposts under command of a sergeant or junior officer, who would be sent to man high ground on the outskirts of Ladysmith during the siege. Their task was to give early warning of any move by the enemy. Even a small rocky outcrop such as Waggon Hill, pictured here, would give excellent visibility over great distances. This would allow most of the picquet to rest while two or three of their number kept watch.

battalion spent four months in Ladysmith besieged by the Boers. More than half the battalion was captured after a night operation to seize a ridge outside the town went badly wrong, through no fault of the 28th.

Fortunately the tide soon turned. The stubborn defence by the garrisons in Ladysmith, Mafeking and Kimberley fired public imagination. Lord Roberts was appointed Commander-in-Chief and dispatched to South Africa with fresh troops, including the 61st. A rapid campaign of forced marches followed in February 1900. On short rations with light kit and little rest, often covering over twenty miles a day, the 61st was part of the force which caught up with and surrounded the Boers at Paardeberg. Fierce fighting followed, and after nine days the Boers surrendered. The 61st was detached to escort 4,000 Boer prisoners to the rear and the 28th was avenged. Two weeks later, after many actions and more marching, weather-beaten, lean and no doubt very hungry, the 61st entered Bloemfontein in triumph with the remainder of its division.

The 28th was reunited when Pretoria was captured and the prisoners were released. After a few months' rest they were sent to Ceylon, guarding their former captors. From both battalions, around 350 officers and men died in the Boer War, 250 of them from disease. The Volunteer battalions had played their part too; many individuals served in the ranks of the 61st. The 4th Battalion, the former Royal North Gloucestershire Militia, was embodied during the war and relieved the 61st in Ireland. After the Paardeberg victory, it was decided to send Boer prisoners to

After the surrender of the main Boer Army, the 61st were part of the force which captured Bloemfontein, capital of the Orange Free State. They remained there for four years on garrison duty and are pictured here in 1900. The officer wearing a helmet is Lieutenant D. Burges who won the Victoria Cross in the Balkans in 1918.

The 4th Glosters (Militia) seen escorting Boer prisoners of war after their disembarkation in St Helena in April 1900. After a month at sea on their journey from Ireland, the march up the steep hill from the dockside was hard work, carrying arms, accoutrements and ammunition. They are headed by William of Gloucester, the Battalion's pet goat.

The Boer prisoners on St Helena filled their time carving ornaments, canes and other souvenirs which they sold to their guards for pocket money. Several of these items, brought home by men of the 4th Glosters, may be seen in the Regimental Museum in Gloucester today.

the lonely Atlantic island of St Helena. The 4th Battalion, having volunteered to serve anywhere, went to guard them for over a year before returning to Cirencester in 1901.

THE FIRST WORLD WAR: 1914–1918

The Boer War revealed defects in the Victorian military system. Equipment, tactics and training were all sadly inadequate for war in the early 20th century. By 1914, when the First World War began, many reforms had been carried out. The army was reorganized, re-equipped and its training methods overhauled. Greater emphasis was placed upon marksmanship, fitness and manoeuvre. A General Staff was formed to provide more professional direction; an Expeditionary Force was organized and the Territorial Army was created as a reserve for the regular army. The official historian of the Great War was probably right to describe the British Expeditionary Force of August 1914, which included the 28th, as 'incomparably the best trained, best organized and best equipped British Army that ever went forth to war'. It was also very small. After the initial flurry of manoeuvre by the Allied armies which halted the German advance, the front stabilized. The 61st, hurried home from China, reached France in December. In March 1915 the territorial battalions of the regiment arrived – the 1st/4th (City of Bristol), 1st/5th and 1st/6th Battalions.[1]

At the outbreak of the First World War, Lord Kitchener asked for 100,000 volunteers. The recruiting offices were besieged, as 500,000 men answered the call. Whole work forces volunteered *en masse*, as did these employees of the Stroud Brewery, many of whom served in the Glosters. Most thought it would be a short war. Britain eventually needed 5 million men before the Armistice in 1918.

A group of the 61st in Flanders early in the First World War. Men lived, rested, ate, sheltered and, all too often, died in the line of entrenchments such as this which, by autumn 1914, stretched from the Alps to the Channel.

Men in the trenches were vulnerable to enemy sniper fire if they exposed their heads above the parapet. Ingenious inventors sought a solution to the problem. Here Company Sergeant Major Tibbles of 1st/5th Glosters tests a French periscopic rifle whilst a corporal spots the results with binoculars through a carefully concealed peephole. The shorts indicate very hot weather.

Months of artillery bombardment had churned the Somme by the winter of 1916/17 into an impenetrable morass in the no man's land between the opposing lines of trenches. Men drowned in the rain-filled shell holes, and movement floundered to a halt in the quagmire. Conditions like these made the life of the defender a misery, and that of the attacker suicidal.

Only twenty miles behind the Somme battlefield, French farmers continue to make hay in the peaceful countryside.

A group from 144 Brigade, who had been grouped together as a light trench mortar brigade, including men of 1st/4th (City of Bristol) and 1st/6th Glosters with a display of captured enemy headgear. The German spiked helmets were prized items of booty.

Private Leslie Cowley of the 5th Glosters with other disabled veterans of the First World War in their distinctive military hospital uniforms with bright red ties. Soon he will be fitted with an artificial limb and will go home to his family. For him the war, but not the suffering, is over. He eventually lived to the age of 85, dying in 1983.
Courtesy of Mrs Louise Walker

Work begins on a line of entrenchments on the Balkan Front in 1916. The 2nd Battalion fought in Macedonia from 1916 to 1918 against the Germans and their Austrian, Hungarian and Bulgarian allies.

The early British tanks had a crew of eight and travelled at 3.7 m.p.h. Their first appearance
in 1916 astounded the infantry on both sides. Tanks were the first serious attempt to restore
mobility to the battlefield by crushing machine-gun posts without exposing attacking troops
to enemy fire. To begin with they were few in number and unreliable, thus achieving little.
Nonetheless this disabled German monster was sufficiently impressive to be included in one
Gloster's private collection of wartime snaps.

After the war, there was some criticism of Allied Generals who based themselves in
comfortable chateaux whilst their troops suffered in the trenches. Certainly it was difficult
for staff officers based in such cloistered calm to keep in touch with the reality of conditions
in the front line. However, lack of radio and dependence upon fixed telephone lines made
the movement of headquarters difficult. The picture shows the HQ of General Gough's 5th
Army on the Ypres Front in late 1917.

The town of Albert lay just behind the Somme battlefield, at times within range of German artillery. Atop the cathedral tower, the giant statue of the Blessed Virgin and Child was hit and knocked over. Defying all the efforts of the German gunners to dislodge it, the statue was a familiar sight to Glosters passing on their way to the front. A superstition grew among the French that the fall of the statue would be a signal for the downfall of the enemy. In the spring offensive of 1918, the Germans recaptured Albert and 'the Lady' was brought down by British artillery. Seven months later, the war was over.

Two Glosters of the 1st/4th Territorial Battalion (Bristol's Own) somewhere in Flanders. On the right is Company Sergeant Major Will Bizley. He was mentioned in despatches for bravery in 1916 but was subsequently wounded and captured by the Germans. He survived the war.
Courtesy of Mr W. Merrett

By 1918, the Gloucestershire Regiment had raised twenty-four battalions. For the first two years, all were volunteers, the cream of the county's youth. Not until 1916, in response to the rising casualty toll, was universal conscription introduced. Sixteen battalions fought in France and Flanders and, as other theatres of war developed, in Italy, Gallipoli, Egypt, Mesopotamia, Persia or Macedonia. The Regiment won seventy-two new battle honours, but 8,100 Glosters lost their lives.

Although photography was well developed by the time war came, many of the pictures taken were not seen by the public until years later, sometimes with the caveat that 'they should not be put into the hands of children'. Early in the war, a series of books, illustrated with heroic paintings, was entitled *Deeds that Thrill the Empire*. It drew heavily upon the published citations for gallantry decorations, such as the Distinguished Conduct Medal awarded to Lance-Corporal F.W. Harvey of the 2nd/5th Glosters after a daring patrol action in August 1915 in the 'no-man's land' between the opposing lines of trenches.

Apart from the opening and closing stages of the war, stalemate superseded manoeuvre. Accurate machine-guns and powerful artillery stifled all attempts at breakthrough. Wireless was in its infancy and, lacking reliable communications,

When the First World War began, Company Sergeant Major William Biddle was a private soldier, the signalling storeman in the 1st Battalion. After the war, his commanding officer noted: 'The war proved him to be a real leader of men as well as a most courageous fighter.' By 1918 he had been awarded the Military Cross, the Distinguished Conduct Medal (twice) and the Military Medal (twice) for gallantry. He is believed to be one of the most decorated men in the history of the British Army. He is seen here with his family after receiving the MC in 1917 from King George V. Having survived the First World War, Biddle was killed while watching an air raid in Clacton during the Second World War.

A total of five Victoria Crosses were awarded to members of the Regiment during the First World War. Two of them are shown here.

In August 1917, Second-Lieutenant H.F. Parsons from Bristol (left), newly commissioned in 14th Glosters, was commanding a trench outpost which was attacked. Although severely wounded by enemy fire bombs he delayed the Germans by throwing grenades until reinforcements arrived. He subsequently died from his wounds.

In October 1918, Private F.G. Miles from the Forest of Dean, a member of 1st/5th Glosters, distinguished himself under heavy fire when, single-handed, he neutralized the enemy machine-guns by killing the gunners and capturing the crews. His signals then allowed his company to outflank the remaining enemy positions and capture a further sixteen guns and fifty-one enemy soldiers. Private Miles is shown here (below) receiving his Victoria Cross in front of his comrades.

commanders were dependent upon fixed telephone lines or runners for information. When the lines were cut or the runner, if he got through at all, was delayed, then late or inaccurate information led to flawed plans. Even when commanders knew what had to be done, they often lacked the means to do it. Barbed wire, shellfire and the mud that permeated everything hindered the movement of reserves. Such obstacles were not to be overcome until the arrival of the tank restored the mobility and protection needed to allow the exploitation of the infantry's hard won gains.

The Glosters came to know these conditions well. The 'trenches' epitomized the experience of all who fought in the Great War. The pictures in this book can give little more than an impression of the conditions, characterized by discomfort, broken sleep, rats, lice and the foul odours of latrine buckets, unwashed feet and decomposing bodies. Often the distance from regimental cooks precluded hot meals and the staple front trench diet was bully beef, rock-hard biscuits, plum and apple jam and tea. The occasional rum issue provided a mild diversion. To modern generations it seems incredible that men could do their duty and survive under these conditions while retaining their sanity. That most did so and kept their sense of humour is a tribute to the strength of the regimental system and the innate patient, stolid endurance of the soldiers.

It was left to the soldiers to express in verse their view of life at the front, the terrors of the great battles and the frightful casualties. Two notable poets served in the ranks of the Glosters; Ivor Gurney and the same F.W. Harvey whose gallantry was described earlier. In company with most veterans, both were critical of hypocritical 'armchair experts' viewing the war from the comfort of their firesides:

> We have taken a trench
> Near Combles, I see,
> Along with the French.
>
> We have taken a trench.
> (Oh, the bodies, the stench!)
> Won't you have some more tea?
> We have taken a trench
> Near Combles, I see.

F.W. Harvey DCM late 1st/5th Glosters
At Afternoon Tea – Triolet

One memorable regimental action took place in April 1918 at the battle of Festubert. The Germans had launched a final desperate offensive to break through the British lines and reach the Channel ports. Festubert was a pivot of the British defence, held by the 28th. The enemy infiltrated to the flanks and rear of the battalion, which was soon attacked on all sides by up to four regiments. In a fight reminiscent of that at Alexandria, the Glosters defended their positions with such tenacity that the German attack failed. Nowhere did they get into the battalion's trenches. The number of decorations awarded to the Glosters, including twenty-five Military Medals, is believed to be a record for a single day's fighting.

THE SECOND WORLD WAR: 1939–1945

The First World War was portrayed as 'The War to End All Wars', but by the late 1930s, with the growth of Fascism and the rise of Hitler in Germany, the war clouds were gathering over Europe again. The 2nd Battalion had received a foretaste of what was to come when, in 1936, they were hastily mobilized and spent a year in Egypt guarding the frontier with Libya, then threatened by Mussolini's fascist army.

By 1937, rearmament was under way. Two territorial battalions were converted to other arms; the 4th (City of Bristol) Battalion became an anti-aircraft, artillery searchlight unit whilst the 6th Battalion was turned into the 44th Royal Tank Regiment. In 1938 the Territorial Army was doubled overnight and a new 7th Battalion of the regiment was raised. By September 1939, the 1st Glosters were in Burma, while the 2nd Battalion was at home in Plymouth.

When war broke out, the 2nd Glosters went to France with the British Expeditionary Force. They were followed by the 5th Battalion and, by the time the Germans invaded the Low Countries in May 1940, both battalions were part of the force which moved into Belgium. With the collapse of the French army they were soon in the thick of the fighting during the subsequent withdrawal.

By late May 1940, both battalions were ordered to defend the Dunkirk approaches to cover the evacuation of the BEF. At a critical stage of the battle, the 2nd Glosters held the small town of Cassel for four vital days, fighting with great determination despite continued enemy ground assaults and aerial dive bombing. By the time the order to withdraw was given, the battalion was surrounded; the 484 survivors were captured and spent over four years in German prison camps. A few miles away, the 5th Battalion put up equally fierce resistance at Ledringhem. Fortunately, it was ordered to withdraw earlier and the remnants of the battalion were evacuated from the Dunkirk beaches.

Meanwhile the old 28th, the 1st Battalion, was still in the Far East. It had left England in 1928 and, its strength sustained by drafts from the 61st, had served in Egypt, Singapore and India before moving to Burma in 1938. The soldiers' families and all the regiment's possessions, including the Colours and the regimental silver, were with them. The evacuation of the families after Japan entered the war in 1941 is described in Chapter 5. When the Japanese, with the advantage of numbers, invaded Burma in early 1942, the ill-equipped, dispersed British garrison was forced to withdraw.

During the long retreat to the Indian frontier, the 28th became the rear guard. They fought fierce actions at Letpadan, Paungde and Shwedaung to check, harry and delay the Japanese advance. The action at Letpadan, although small, was one of the first reverses suffered by the Japanese and delayed them in that area for a week. Amongst others, it provoked a message of congratulation from Her Majesty Queen Mary, then living in Badminton and guarded by a company of 8th Glosters.

The retreat, which had begun in March 1942, ended in June when the 28th reached India. The battalion had covered over 600 miles at the cost of 164 Glosters killed. During the retreat, they had been forced to bury most of the regimental silver, although some small items were carried out by individuals who found room in their small packs for treasured regimental heirlooms. Later in the war, a search party returned to the burial site but found it disturbed and the silver missing. Some items were found nearby but most would never be seen again.

At the outbreak of the Second World War, recruits for the Glosters were still trained at the regimental depot in Horfield Barracks, Bristol. These recruits are dressed in the new battledress but their ammunition pouches date from the 1920s.

Cigarettes for the troops, presented by the Gloucester *Citizen* arriving at the Battalion HQ of 7th Glosters in Gloucester, December 1939. The 7th Battalion was a territorial unit of the regiment, raised in 1938 and mobilized in 1939. In 1940 they went to Northern Ireland to train for three years before returning to England to prepare for the invasion of France. In 1944, they were disappointed to hear that their division was not to take part in the invasion and they became a training unit.

The 8th Battalion was formed in 1940, and was employed on defence duties in England. One company guarded Badminton House between 1940–42, where Queen Mary was a reluctant evacuee from London and a guest of the Duke of Beaufort. Her Majesty took a great interest in the men and their welfare. She took a particular delight in wearing the back badge when visiting the troops.

A mechanized column of the 1st Battalion carries out final checks before moving off to fight the Japanese in Rangoon, January 1942. Bren gun carriers of the type in the foreground were to play an important role in smashing through Japanese road blocks. The motor-cyclist despatch rider wears a pith helmet – steel helmets were in short supply.

British Paramount News captured this shot of the 28th holding the railway line near Toungoo in Southern Burma in March 1942. Shortly afterwards the Commanding Officer, Lieutenant-Colonel Bagot, was wounded and his second-in-command was killed. Much desperate fighting followed.

Most of the silver of the 28th, much of it Georgian, was buried in the withdrawal from Burma and never recovered. One of the four candelabra was found in Malaya in 1965, its identity established from this photograph, taken in Cologne in 1922.

Yenangyaung, on the banks of the Irrawaddy, was one of the richest areas in the world in 1942. There were 5,000 oil wells, three petrol refineries and the largest power station in Burma. Since oil was vital to the Japanese it was necessary to deny it to the enemy. As the Japanese drew nearer the facilities had to be destroyed. The 28th were ordered to cover the demolitions. Private Field can be seen smashing electrical machinery whilst million gallon oil tanks are ablaze in the background.

A territorial battalion of the regiment, the 10th Glosters, achieved great distinction in the recapture of Burma from the Japanese during 1944–5. Here they advance past a battle-scarred Burmese temple.

10th Glosters fought in many sharp actions against the Japanese in the thick Burmese jungle. Here, Major Pope of D Company proudly displays a sword captured from the enemy.

Lord Louis Mountbatten, Allied Commander, speaks to 10th Glosters in Burma, 1945. The back badge is evident on the Glosters' Australian-style slouch hats. Made popular by Field Marshal Slim, they became a common form of headgear in the closing stages of the war in Burma.

Officers of the 2nd and 5th Battalions who were captured in the rearguard action before Dunkirk in 1940 spent the rest of the war behind barbed wire in German POW camps. They were separated from their men in special Offizierlager (Officer Camps). Not required to work by the Geneva Convention, boredom was rife. Many made plans for escape and some were successful. In the meantime, diversions such as the camp orchestra helped to pass the time.

During the Second World War, nineteen battalions of the Home Guard were raised in the regiment, ten in the county and nine in Bristol and Avonmouth, numbering over 27,000 men and women at their peak. Sergeant B. Stanley-Clarke served in the 1st Gloucestershire (Cheltenham) Home Guard Battalion. She had two cousins in the Glosters, one of whom, Captain R.A. St M. Reeve-Tucker was killed in action in Korea.

The 2nd Battalion landed in Normandy on D-Day, 6 June 1944, without great loss and reached Bayeux the next day. During the following week they were involved in the fighting in the *bocage* countryside of Normandy. The photograph of a German Panther tank destroyed during an attack by the 61st was taken during an operation to secure the village of Lingevres on 13 June.

Back in England, the 61st had reformed from a cadre of the old battalion and was brought up to strength again. Other battalions of the regiment had also been raised. Apart from the 8th (Home Service) Battalion, there were also 7th, 9th, 10th, 11th and 70th (Young Soldiers) units. In this war, fewer infantry were required than during 1914–18 and several wartime battalions were converted to other cap badges or drafted as individual reinforcements. The 10th Battalion was an exception. Despite having been trained as a tank battalion, they saw active service as infantry in the Far East from 1944. Both on the Arakan front and later during the victorious advance to recapture Burma, they earned a high reputation, distinguishing themselves at Pinwe and Myitson.

Both the 2nd and the 5th Battalion returned to France in the Normandy landings. The 5th Glosters became the spearhead reconnaissance unit of the 43rd Wessex Division and fought many brave actions up to and beyond the Rhine. The 61st in France was in the forefront during the capture of Le Havre and in April 1945 led the operations to capture Arnhem. When the Germans surrendered three weeks later, the Glosters moved forward to Soest in Germany. In Soest the 61st were inspected by Field Marshal Montgomery, and were able to produce ten serving holders of the Military Medal to meet him.

Le Havre was one of the strongest German fortresses of the Atlantic Wall with elaborate concrete defences, minefields and other obstacles. It was captured by the 49th Division after thirty-six hours' fighting in which the 2nd Battalion played a prominent part. Here B Company enter the town on 12 September 1944, severely damaged by RAF bombing. Every man carries a spade on his back in order to be able to dig in against enemy counter attacks. The slogan 'dig or die' was taken very seriously.

THE KOREAN WAR: 1950–3

The Glosters were in Colchester in 1950 when, half a world away, communist North Korea invaded South Korea and the United Nations decided to send a force to resist them. The battalion contained both regular and National Servicemen serving their obligatory two years' conscription. They were brought up to war strength with reservists, including war veterans, who were recalled with varying degrees of enthusiasm. By October 1950, after intensive training, they sailed for Korea to join the British 29th Independent Infantry Brigade.

Initially, the UN had been forced to retreat but, when the Glosters arrived in November, they had regained the initiative and were advancing northwards. 29th Brigade was ordered to seek out enemy guerrilla bands cut off by the UN advance. Many believed that the war would be over by Christmas.

Although the Glosters didn't realize it then, the prospect of early return had receded rapidly when the Chinese Communists joined the war as allies of North Korea. By December 1950, Chinese forces were actively engaged and the UN suffered fresh setbacks. It was a confusing period for the battalion; digging countless positions, then moving on before finishing them without a sign of the enemy.

The 28th/61st embark for Korea aboard HM Troopship *Empire Windrush* at Southampton in October 1950. Two months earlier, one-third of the battalion had been civilians; ex-soldiers with a reserve liability who were recalled for service when South Korea was invaded. After three weeks of intensive training and two weeks' embarkation leave, they were off to war. As they boarded, the regimental band played *Far Away Places*.

Their first test came in February 1951 when ordered to capture a high, steep feature marked on the maps as *Hill 327*. By evening, after a fierce struggle, the hill was in Gloster hands. Their baptism by fire was over, but a sterner trial was yet to come.

By early April, the 28th/61st were defending a seven-mile front along the Imjin River, astride the historic invasion route to Seoul, the South Korean capital thirty miles south. So few troops were available that, on either flank, their nearest neighbours were several miles distant. Information on the enemy was sketchy, although intelligence suggested an imminent Chinese offensive. Yet long range patrols north of the Imjin reported no sign of the Chinese, apart from occasional observation posts.

To block enemy progress, the Glosters were forced to disperse their defences on high ground about a mile from the Imjin. Gaps between positions were covered by observation and machine-gun, mortar or artillery fire. There were few obstacles to

Lieutenant-Colonel J.P. Carne VC, DSO: the calm, reassuring figure of the Commanding Officer of the Glosters. 'Lieutenant-Colonel Carne showed powers of leadership which can seldom have been surpassed in the history of our Army. He inspired his officers and men to fight beyond the normal limits of human endurance, in spite of overwhelming odds and ever increasing casualties, shortage of ammunition and water.' (From the official citation for the Victoria Cross awarded to Lt. Col. Carne.)

At the foot of Castle Hill, where A Company came under heavy Chinese attack on 23 April, the day after this photograph was taken. Lieutenant Philip Curtis (left) was later awarded a posthumous Victoria Cross. Second-Lieutenant Terence Waters was to die in captivity and was awarded a posthumous George Cross.

Burnt-out battalion vehicles in the area of the original Glosters' HQ. Above them, the precipitous heights of Hill 235 upon which the surviving defenders concentrated for the final phase of the Imjin battle. One of the battalion, upon hearing from the CO that they were to move up there said cheerfully, 'We'll be all right, sir. 'Twill be like the Rock of Gibraltar up here.'

Attempts by the United Nations to break through and relieve the Glosters on the Imjin failed when tanks of the relief column were destroyed by the Chinese, blocking the only route forward through this defile. All other attempts at relief failed and the Glosters were cut off.

The rugged, inhospitable hills of South Korea saw much bitter fighting between 22 and 25 April 1951. This scene, taken after the battle, looks south from the forward positions on Castle Hill. Second-Lieutenant Denys Whatmore, a survivor of the battle, points out the historic invasion route astride which the 28th/61st fought. To the right is Hill 235, later known as Gloster Hill. Here the beleaguered remnants of the battalion made their final stand.

About 450 Glosters were captured by the Chinese after the battle of the Imjin. They endured a nightmare march of over 300 miles northwards, carrying their wounded. A number died *en route*. No news was heard of them until this photograph was released by the Chinese some months later. For some families this picture was the first indication that those posted missing remained alive.

slow any enemy advance, particularly the massed attacks favoured by the Chinese; barbed wire and mines were in short supply.

On 22 April, shortly after noon, artillery observation posts spotted Chinese troops north of the river, near a ford nicknamed Gloster Crossing.[2] That night, a platoon ambush was laid on the crossing to prevent the Chinese from crossing the moonlit Imjin. Shortly after dusk, they annihilated the enemy's advance party. Four separate assaults were beaten off with many enemy casualties and no loss to the Glosters who, with ammunition low, were withdrawn.

By now, the Chinese were crossing the Imjin in several places and attacked the forward positions. On the left flank, A Company on Castle Hill bore the brunt of the enemy's assault. Outnumbered six to one, after six hours' fighting, much of it hand to hand, they were driven back. At dawn, the UN's superior air power might have made a difference, but none was available.

Lieutenant Philip Curtis won a posthumous Victoria Cross leading his platoon in a counter attack to recover Castle Hill. Early on he was wounded, but refused treatment, mounting a single-handed assault on a Chinese machine-gun post, destroying it with grenades. In the process, he was killed and although Castle Hill was not retaken, A Company's furious reaction to the Chinese attack produced a valuable pause in the battle.

Early on 23 April, the forward positions were becoming untenable. Those to the rear were also under heavy attack, almost overwhelmed by sheer weight of numbers. The gaps between positions grew wider and, without air support, each was at risk of being isolated and destroyed. Some wounded were evacuated, but by noon the Chinese had blocked the tracks to the rear. Several attempts to fight through to relieve the Glosters failed. Meanwhile, units on the Glosters' flanks had been forced back and the battalion was cut off.

Further attacks took place that night, forcing the battalion into a tighter defensive perimeter. Shortly after dawn on 24 April, all were in new positions on a steep, rugged feature called *Hill 235*. Meanwhile, the Brigade Commander stressed that the battalion must stand firm; unrestricted passage of the Chinese past the Glosters would lead to the whole division being cut off. The battalion was now reduced to a fighting strength of about 350, short of food, ammunition, radio batteries and water.

Early on 25 April, waves of determined Chinese attacked the hill, indifferent to their casualties and directed by cacophonous trumpets. To confuse them, the Adjutant ordered the Drum Major to sound his bugle and play all known British calls – except Retreat. Apparently surprised, Chinese movement stopped for a while. The attacks began again after dawn; seven assaults were repulsed within one hour. Finally air support arrived, and a series of rocket, napalm and machine-gun strikes brought some respite.

Relief was clearly impossible and the brigade commander authorized the battalion to try and fight its way out with artillery support. By the time scheduled for breakout, the CO heard that the guns could not help; they were under attack themselves. The orders to the Glosters were now quite simple – every man to make his own way back. Back at Brigade HQ, the brigadier wrote in the log, in his own hand, 'No-one but the Glosters could have done this.'

Splitting into small groups, they tried to work their way back to the UN lines, now seven miles away. The intervening landscape swarmed with Chinese troops

When Lieutenant-Colonel Carne was captured, his second-in-command, Digby Grist, himself wounded in the battle, took over. Here Lieutenant-Colonel Grist gives men of 2nd Battalion, The Royal Canadian Regiment, an account of the fighting. The Glosters have a happy association with the RCR dating from 1925 and regularly exchange officers. Seated beside Colonel Grist is Captain Mike Harvey. He led eighty-one of his men in a hazardous and circuitous escape from the Chinese after the Imjin battle. Forty-one reached safety, sixteen of whom were wounded. Captain Harvey was subsequently awarded the Military Cross.

and most Glosters were captured or killed. Only one small party, under Captain Mike Harvey, reached safety. Of those on the strength of the battalion on 22 April, 297 remained by the 26th. Sixty-three had been killed in action and forty-six had been evacuated wounded. The remainder were missing. Although some rejoined later, most were in Chinese hands and would remain in captivity until August 1953.

Many survivors spoke later of their confidence that they could cope, despite the mounting casualties, shrinking perimeter and dwindling ammunition. That the battalion remained a fighting entity right to the end, owed much to the confidence inspired by the courage and cool leadership of the commanding officer. Lieutenant-Colonel Carne went into captivity with his men and survived harsh treatment while imprisoned. He was subsequently awarded the Victoria Cross in recognition of his brave and distinguished conduct. The 28th/61st was awarded America's highest award for collective gallantry – the US Presidential Distinguished Unit Citation. Ninety-five Glosters received bravery awards for their part in the battle or the subsequent captivity.

As for the Chinese, their spring offensive had failed. The Chinese 63rd Army had suffered over 11,000 casualties and took no futher part in the war. The front

Sergeant 'Doc' Brisland was Medical Sergeant of the 1st Battalion at the Imjin. When the order to break out was given, he elected to remain behind with the medical officer and the wounded. Later mentioned in despatches for his gallantry, he remained a prisoner of the Chinese for over two years. In September 1953, he was released and returned home to a rapturous welcome from his family. On his sleeve he wears the blue and gold insignia of the US Presidential Citation – a personal award to all those who fought in the battle of the Imjin River. The Citation is now worn by all serving members of the regiment.

stabilized and, in August 1953, a cease-fire was negotiated and the prisoners came home. Thirty-three Glosters had died in the camps from wounds, neglect or starvation. Amongst them was Lieutenant Terry Waters, attached to the 28th/61st from The West Yorkshire Regiment. He had refused treatment for his wounds rather than broadcast propaganda for the enemy. He was later awarded a posthumous George Cross.

Chapter 8

EPILOGUE

Here's a health to every brother in arms –
Safe returned from war's alarms;
Maimed and merry, hale and bold,
To pledge our fellowship of old.

And now (in silence) another toast
To gallant friends – a mighty host
Asleep with foreign earth for bed,
Till Doomsday reveille – the Glorious Dead.

F.W. Harvey DCM, late 5th Glosters

After the Imjin Battle, the battalion reformed under the energetic leadership of the second-in-command. Gathering in survivors and all available reinforcements, Major Digby Grist signalled the Colonel-in-Chief, ' . . . we are operational again.' The Glosters took their place in the line once more, in a quiet sector while they were re-equipped. Major Grist was promoted, confirmed in command and, in December 1951, brought the battalion home.[1]

Bidding farewell to the reservists, recalled for Korea, the Glosters began a new chapter in their history at the School of Infantry in Wiltshire. In 1952, they laid up their old Colours in Gloucester Cathedral, receiving replacements from their Colonel-in-Chief, HRH The Duke of Gloucester. In June 1953, in heavy rain, while the battalion lined part of the route, the band led the Coronation procession of the new Queen from Westminster Abbey.

In December 1954, the regiment sailed for foreign parts once more. It spent over three years engaged in counter terrorist and internal security operations during the Mau-Mau rebellion in Kenya, as well as in Aden, Bahrain and the EOKA terrorist campaign in Cyprus. At this time around two-thirds of the battalion was National Servicemen.

The 28th/61st returned to England in 1958 and received the Freedom of the City of Bristol, an honour also conferred upon them by the City of Gloucester in 1946. The award of a Freedom is a mark of especial recognition by the local community. It acknowledges the close ties existing between the regiment and the people of Gloucestershire and Bristol since the eighteenth century. As a sign of the trust reposed in the regiment by the population, the Glosters are permitted to exercise

Field Marshal Lord Roberts VC unveils in 1905 the memorial in Bristol to the Glosters who fought and died in the Boer War.

They shall grow not old as we that are left grow old
Age shall not weary them, nor the years condemn.
At the going down of the sun and in the morning
We will remember them.

The dedication of the regimental memorial in Gloucester Park in 1925. It was subscribed by the Territorial 1st/5th and 2nd/5th Glosters in memory of those members of the regiment who died in the First World War. Both battalions recruited mainly from the Gloucester and Cheltenham area.

Lieutenant Manley James VC, MC, shown here at the Armistice Day parade in 1923, was awarded the Victoria Cross for conspicuous bravery and devotion to duty over a period of four days in April 1918 during the battle of St Quentin in France. As a company commander in 8th Glosters, in the wartime rank of captain, he led his company with great determination and courage in several actions over four days despite being wounded twice. On the final day, during a local counter-attack on his own initiative, he was wounded a third time and was last seen working a machine-gun single-handed. He was widely believed to have been killed but was taken prisoner and survived his wounds. After the war he reverted to his peacetime rank of lieutenant.

Remembrance Day was originally named after the signing of the Armistice which ended the First World War, and is commemorated at 11 a.m. on the eleventh day of the eleventh month every year in memory of the sacrifice of those who died in all wars.

the privilege of marching through the streets with 'drums beating, Colours flying and bayonets fixed'. In later years the Glosters were to be granted the Freedom of Cheltenham, Tewkesbury Borough, the Forest of Dean and the districts of Stroud, the Cotswolds and North Avon.

Another tour in England, after 1960, saw the phasing out of National Service conscription. It was an all-volunteer, regular battalion that sailed for Cyprus aboard the SS *Nevasa* in March 1962, on one of the last troopship voyages to the Mediterranean. Thereafter, all overseas moves would take place by air and so another era came to an end. In the ensuing years the battalion would return to Cyprus again as part of the United Nations peace-keeping force. It has also served in Swaziland, Bechuanaland, Basutoland, Mauritius, and once more in Aden.

In 1967, the last remaining territorial battalion of the Regiment, the Fifth, was disbanded as part of a radical reorganization of the TA. Their successors are the men and women of The Wessex Regiment (Rifle Volunteers) based in Gloucester, Cheltenham, Bristol and the Forest of Dean.

In 1969, the battalion was sent on the first of many tours of duty to help maintain law and order in the troubled province of Ulster. In the process, some Glosters have been wounded or lost their lives, the first casualties since Korea. Fortunately, rather more have been decorated for gallantry or meritorious service. Apart from active service in Northern Ireland, the battalion has been stationed several times in West Germany, as part of the British Army of the Rhine, and twice in Berlin. Three times since 1945, the battalion has served in Central America to deter Guatemalan threats against the tiny Caribbean state of Belize.

In 1990, the 28th/61st returned from yet another tour in Ulster to form part of the 24th Airmobile Brigade, stationed at Catterick in North Yorkshire. It is there that this story ends, as the Glosters look forward with their customary steadfastness and good humour to whatever the future holds for them.

In these pages we have tried to illustrate, with photographs, the special ties that exist between the men and families of regiments such as the Glosters, and their county. Such links draw men together in peace, and in war can inspire them to extraordinary feats of human achievement despite fearful odds. The regimental war memorials and headstones in Bristol, Gloucestershire and every continent bear silent witness to the courage and sacrifice of Glosters over the centuries since 1694.

West Countrymen rarely speak of loyalty and fidelity, but such concepts are second nature to the Glosters. Badges, battle honours and uniforms are important, but the story of this regiment is underpinned more by the indomitable spirit of its soldiers than anything else. That spirit is born of shared joys and hardships, not always in equal measure. These common experiences are recalled with feeling at annual reunions, remembering times in Burma, India, Germany, Ireland, Korea or elsewhere. Those who have not been part of the family cannot fully understand the comradeship and devotion that men of the regiment feel for each other. Their quiet pride in the Glosters and its record in good times and bad transcends time and has led successive kin to join their county regiment. The names of those with generations of service appear regularly throughout the pages of the regimental journals: Arengo-Jones, Baker, Barlow, Boon, Brackenbury, Brisland, Brushneen, Burges, Burnside, Chapman, Danahy, Deacon, Dutton, Falkiner, Firth, Grazebrook, Grist, James, Kibble, Ladds, McLeod, Mirehouse, Musto, Potter, Radice, Read, Ruddy, Scaife, Vicary, Waters and Wilkinson . . . There are many others since, first and foremost, the Glosters were and are a family regiment.

> O God, whose face is against them that do evil,
> Grant that we, Thy servants of The Gloucestershire Regiment,
> May ever stand back to back against all evils that beset us,
> And never turning our backs to Thee,
> May steadfastly behold Thy glory
> In the face of Jesus Christ, Our Saviour.
>
> Amen[2]

NOTES

Introduction

1.   Two such early nineteenth-century artists who served in the 61st Regiment were Private Porter (Egypt 1801) and Lieutenant-Colonel Deacon who saw service in the Sikh Wars and the Indian Mutiny.

Chapter 1

1.   See *Men Against Fire*, Gen. S.L.A. Marshall (William Morrow, 1947) – an interesting study by an American General of the performance of US soldiers in battle during the Second World War.
2.   *The Armies of Britain, 1485–1980*, Michael Barthorp (The National Army Museum & Seagull SA, Guernsey, C.I., 1980).
3.   *Cap of Honour*, D. Scott Daniell (1951); see also Chapter 5, for the story of Sergeant Ball's wife.
4.   For a fuller explanation of the system of battle honours, see Chapter 3.

Chapter 2

1.   *An Anthology of Military Quotations*, Michael Dewar. (Robert Hale, 1990). (1990).
2.   A fuller description of the part played by the families in regimental life, and the hardships they endured with their menfolk, may be found in Chapter 5.
3.   The old Duke of Wellington is alleged to have said, 'By Jove!, if ever there is a mutiny in the army – and in all probability we shall have one – you'll see that these new-fangled school masters will be at the bottom of it!' *The British Soldier: His Life from Tudor to Modern Times*, Colonel H. de Watteville (1954).
4.   Straw-filled paliasses were still in use in the British Army, albeit in short term training camps, in Germany in the mid-1970s.
5.   Regimental Sergeant-Major G. Pearce who served between 1918 and 1945, quoted in *Memories of the Old and Bold – The Soldiers Memories*, a collection of soldiers' letters edited by Brigadier P.C.S. Heidenstam (The Gloucestershire Regiment, 1990).
6.   Despite their new title, members of both battalions continued to refer to themselves as being of the 28th or the 61st. Either title was interchangeable.

Chapter 4

1. Unpublished journal of Lieutenant-Colonel E. Charlton, 61st Foot (Gloucestershire Regimental Archives).
2. *Cap of Honour*, D. Scott Daniell (1951).
3. The Calcutta Cup was given to the Calcutta Rugby Club by the Rugby Football Union in return for the cup of the same name which had been presented by the citizens of Calcutta, primarily Scots and English, for annual competition between Scotland and England. Its Indian counterpart was one of the premier competitions in India.
4. Navy, Army and Air Force institutes were formed after the First World War, and apart from providing a canteen were eventually expanded to include recreation, reading rooms and a Corporals' Club. Small shops which sold soldiers' necessaries and household items for the families were also added.
5. Tea and buns.
6. Married men were similarly privileged. The social activities of both officers and men played a prominent part in regimental life. See Chapter 5.
7. Tea.
8. Laundry.
9. *Memories of the Old and Bold.*

Chapter 5

1. Both quotations are cited in *Judy Grady & The Colonel's Lady*, Noel St John Williams (1988), a comprehensive study of the army wife.
2. An extract from army orders of the day, 15 June 1748, reads:

Eleanor Wright, wife of Wm Wright of Bragg's and Anne White tryed for robbing a Bohemian woman is sentenced to receive 20 lashes each by the Common hangman at the head of each Quarter Guard of both lines of British Infantry, and afterwards to be drumm'd out of the Army along the front line by the Drummers of Bragg's Regt with halters about their necks and Labels of their crimes afixed to their Bodies.

3. The same Sergeant Ball whose actions during the Peninsular War are described in Chapter 1.
4. *Cap of Honour*, p. 160.
5. The term 'married families' may seem quaint to modern ears. In part it reflected Victorian concerns for morality. More practically, a soldier was required to accept formal responsibility for his family before he would be allotted married quarters. Even so, for much of the nineteenth century, many marriages were of the common law variety, rather than those with benefit of clergy.
6. RSM G. Pearce (1918–45). From *Memories of the Old and Bold*, op. cit.
7. *On the Strength*, Veronica Banfield (Charles Knight, 1974). Cited by Noel St J. Williams.

Chapter 6

1.   A popular version of this tune is known in Scotland as *The Bannocks of Barley Meal*. Apart from being stationed not far from Kinnegad for a time, the attraction of the tune to the 28th lies in the inclusion of one of their nicknames in the title. During the American Revolution, at the battle of White Plains near New York in 1776, the 28th made vigorous use of their short swords to drive the colonists from their positions and were dubbed 'The Slashers'.

   An alternative version of the nickname's origin stems from Canada in 1764. The 28th were stationed in Montreal where an unpopular merchant, known for his harassment of the soldiers, had on several occasions turned men and their families out of their billets without reason, once in the midst of the severe Canadian winter. One night he was attacked by a group of men in disguise and, during the fracas, half his right ear was cut off. His attackers then withdrew, taking with them the half ear. Although never proven, the 28th were widely held to have been responsible, hence the nickname 'The Slashers'!

2.   Later renamed Robinswood Barracks, it remained as the regimental depot until 1959 when it was closed. Since then, recruits for the regiment have been trained centrally with those of other regiments from Wales and the West in Exeter, Honiton, Crickhowell (Wales) and, currently, Lichfield in Staffordshire.

3.   *Memories of the Old and Bold*.

4.   An Urdu word for 'bed'.

5.   A contemporary account tells us how it was. RSM F.E. Wright describes his recruit training in the winter of 1928/29:

> Of our meagre pay, 2s. 0d. a day, so much went towards cleaning equipment and then deductions for barrack room duties, brickdust for the floor, blacklead and whitewash for coalboxes. It was quite an effort getting ready for inspection, especially on Saturday morning. After the initial sweep-up, brick dust was laid and then the dry scrubber applied. One chap sat on the scrubber and pulled along. The tedious task of scrubbing the table and two forms was performed by taking these outside, irrespective of the weather, and they finished up whiter than white. *Memories of the Old and Bold*.

Chapter 7

1.   The expansion of the wartime army was built on the foundations of the pre-war territorial battalions. When 5th Glosters went to France in September 1914, it was retitled the 1st/5th and a new battalion was formed for Home Service to act as a second line (2nd/5th). With the increasing demand for battalions in Flanders, the distinctions between Home Service battalions and others soon disappeared.

2.   Later, it was discovered that they were the vanguard of the 63rd Chinese Army with three divisions each consisting of roughly 9,000 infantry with their own artillery and mortar support. *Cap of Honour*.

Chapter 8

1.   When the troopship docked in Southampton on 20 December 1951, waiting for Lt. Col. Grist on the quayside were his wife and two sons, one of whom was commissioned into the 28th/61st in 1960. In 1979, Lt. Col. Robin Grist would command the 1st Battalion, and in 1991, having risen to the rank of Major General, was appointed Colonel, The Gloucestershire Regiment.
2.   Regimental Collect of the Glosters (M. Tobias, 1930).

BIBLIOGRAPHY

Barthorp, Michael, *The Armies of Britain, 1485–1980* (National Army Museum & Seagull SA, Guernsey, CI, 1980)

Boden, Anthony, *F.W. Harvey, Soldier, Poet* (Alan Sutton, Gloucester, 1988)

Carew, Tim, *The Glorious Glosters, A Short History of The Gloucestershire Regiment, 1945–1970* (Leo Cooper, 1970)

Cripps, Wilfred and others, *The Royal North Gloucester Militia* (Cirencester, 1914)

Daniell, David Scott, *Cap of Honour: The Story of The Gloucestershire Regiment (28th/61st Foot) 1694–1975* (White Lion Publishers Ltd, 1975)

Dewar, Michael, *An Anthology of Military Quotations* (Robert Hale Ltd, 1990)

Dillon, Terence, *Rangoon to Kohima* (RHQ The Gloucestershire Regiment, Gloucester, 1978)

Featherstone, Donald, F., *All For a Shilling a Day* (Jarrolds, 1966)

Harding, Colonel E.D., *The Imjin Roll* (RHQ The Gloucestershire Regiment, Gloucester, 1976)

Harvey, F.W., *Gloucestershire Friends: Poems from a German Prison Camp* (Sidgwick & Jackson, 1917)

Hastings, Max, *The Korean War* (Guild Publishing, 1987)

Hibbert, Christopher, *The English: A Social History 1066–1945* (Guild Publishing, 1987)

Keegan, John and Holmes, Richard, *Soldiers: A History of Men in Battle* (Hamish Hamilton, 1985)

Kitching, Major General George, *Mud and Green Fields, The Memoirs of General George Kitching* (Battleline Books, Langely, BC, Canada, 1986)

Ministry of Defence, *Trumpet and Bugle Calls for the Army* (HMSO, 1966)

Neuberg, Victor, *Gone For a Soldier: A History of Life in the British Ranks* (Cassell, 1989)

Norman, C.B., *Battle Honours of the British Army: From Tangier 1662 to the Commencement of the Reign of King Edward VII* (David & Charles, Newton Abbot, 1971 reprint of 1911 edition)

Pagan, Brigadier-General A.L.W. *Infantry, An Account of the 1st Gloucestershire Regiment during the War 1914–1918* (Gale & Polden, Aldershot, 1951)

RHQ The Gloucestershire Regiment, *Memories of the Old and Bold, Volume I* (Gloucester, 1987) and *Volume II: The Soldiers Memories* (Gloucester, 1990)

RHQ The Gloucestershire Regiment, *The Slashers: A new short History of The Gloucestershire Regiment (1694–1965)* (Gloucester, 1965)

RHQ The Gloucestershire Regiment, *Never Feared a Foe of Any Kind: The Glosters, 1694–1991* (Gloucester, 1991)

Skelley, Alan Ramsay, *The Victorian Army at Home: The Recruitment and Terms and Conditions of the British Regular, 1859–1899* (McGill–Queen's University Press, Montreal, Canada, 1977)

Terraine, John, *The Western Front, 1914–1918* (Hutchinson, 1964)

Wavell, Field Marshal Earl, *The Good Soldier: A Selection of Essays, Lectures and Articles* (Macmillan, 1948)

Williams, Noel St J., *Judy O'Grady & the Colonel's Lady: The Army Wife and Camp Follower Since 1660* (Brassey's 1988)

INDEX